Paperbacks on Musicology

4

Paperbacks on Musicology
Edited by Andrew D. McCredie
4

HEINRICHSHOFEN EDITION
NEW YORK

WALTER KOLNEDER

Antonio Vivaldi

Documents
of his life and works

Translated by
Kurt Michaelis

HEINRICHSHOFEN EDITION
NEW YORK

Sole Selling Agents:
C.F. Peters Corporation — 373 Park Avenue South, New York, N.Y. 10016

Library of Congress Cataloging in Publication Data

Kolneder, Walter.
  [Antonio Vivaldi, Dokumente seines Lebens und
Schaffens. English]
  Antonio Vivaldi, documents of his life and works.

  (Paperbacks of musicology ; 4)
  Translation of: Antonio Vivaldi, Dokumente seines
Lebens und Schaffens.
  Bibliography: p.
  Includes index.
  1. Vivaldi, Antonio, 1678-1741. 2. Composers—Italy—
Biography. I. Title. II. Series.
ML410.V82K553 1982   780'.92'4 [B]   82-15811

ISBN 3-7959-0338-6 (pbk.)

Contents

78539

Ill. 1: Presumed portrait of Antonio Vivaldi

Antonio (Lucio) Vivaldi

1678-1741

Splendor and misery, oblivion, renaissance

Ill. 2: Title page of the first Bach biography

From c. 1708 on

"Joh. Seb. Bach's initial efforts at composing were imperfect, like all first experiments. He did not receive any lessons which would have given him the direction in which to proceed gradually, step by step, and so he had to take a chance at first, as everybody does who wants to succeed in such an endeavour without guidance. The experiments common to all beginners are to have the hands run up and down on the instrument, to use both hands as much as the five fingers allow and to continue this wild activity until by chance a place is reached to rest. All they will turn out to be is 'finger composers' (or Clavier Husaren [keyboard hussars], as Bach called them in his later years), i.e., they have to let their fingers show them what to write down, instead of dictating to the fingers what they must play. Bach did not persist long on this road. He soon began to feel that the constant running up and down was not enough, that order, connection and relation were needed, and that some kind of instructions were necessary to reach such goals. The violin concertos by Vivaldi, at that time newly published, served him as such instructions. He was so often told about the value of these excellent pieces of music that the happy idea came to him to arrange them all for his clavier. He studied the way the themes were handled, the relations between them, the changes in modulation and many other things, too. The arranging of themes and passages which were written for the violin, but did not fit the clavier, taught him to think musically, so that he did not have to expect ideas from his fingers after finishing work, but could start out by using his own imagination."

(Johann Nikolaus Forkel, Über Johann Sebastian Bachs Leben, Kunst und Kunstwerke, Leipzig 1802, p. 42)

February 27, 1710

Johann Philipp Franz von Erwein, later Prince Bishop of Würzburg, writes to his business friend, the Venetian businessman Regaznig,

". . . to try to get some more rare compositions of Vivaldi and let me have them at the next opportunity . . ."

(Fritz Zobeley: Rudolf Franz Erwein Graf von Schönborn und seine Musikpflege, Würzburg 1949, p. 33)

October 16, 1711

The London newspaper "The Post Man" carries an advertisement about the sale of the 12 Concertos, Op. III "L'Estro Armonico."

1714

In Pirna bekam ich zu dieser Zeit die Vivaldischen Violinenconcerte zum erstenmale zu sehen. Sie machten, als eine damals gantz neue Art von musikalischen Stücken, bey mir einen nicht geringen Eindruck. Ich unterließ nicht, mir davon einen ziemlichen Vorrath zu sammeln. Die prächtigen Ritornelle des Vivaldi, haben mir, in den künftigen Zeiten, zu einem guten Muster gedienet.[+]

Ill. 3: Biographical entry of Johann Joachim Quantz, drafted by himself (from Fr. W. Marpurg: Historisch-Kritische Beyträge zur Aufnahme der Musik, Vol. 1, Berlin 1754/55). Translation see page 198.

February 4, 1715

". . . toward the end, Vivaldi played an accompaniment alone admirably, where he used in the end such imagination that it frightened me quite a bit; it is impossible that anybody ever has played or will play this way, because he got with his fingers so close to the bridge that there was not the width of a straw left and no room for the bow — and this happened on all 4 strings with fugues and at an incredible speed . . ."

(Eberhard Preussner: Die musikalischen Reisen des Herrn von Uffenbach, Kassel 1949, p. 67)

Ill. 4 a/b: *Excerpts from the correspondence of Count Schönborn with the Venetian businessman Regaznig*

1730

"The King (Louis XV.) demanded that the Spring Concerto by Vivaldi be played."
(Mercure de France)

November 16, 1737

"And so I have the honor to correspond with nine Princes and Highnesses; my letters travel all the way across Europe."
Letter by Vivaldi to the Marchese Guido Bentivoglio in Ferrara)

After 1741

"The clergyman Antonio Vivaldi, incomparable violinist, called the Prete rosso, highly esteemed for his operas and concertos, earned during his lifetime more than 50 million ducats, but died, because of great extravagance, a poor man in Vienna."
(Commemoriali Gradenigo, manuscript in the Museo Correr, Venice)

1756

Leopold Mozart's "Attempt at a thorough violin method" appears during the year his son is born; it contains examples by Tartini, but no longer a single one by Vivaldi.

1781

In an Italian music history volume by Saverio Bettinelli the names of Monteverdi and Vivaldi are missing.

1851

"XVI Concertos after violin concertos by Antonio Vivaldi, arranged for piano solo by Johann Sebastian Bach and published for the first time by S. W. Debn and F. A. Roitzsch," are issued by C. F. Peters in Leipzig.

Ill. 5: First edition of J. S. Bach's arrangements after
Vivaldi, Leipzig 1851

S. W. Dehn comments in the preface:
"The original works of Vivaldi have long become musi-
cal rarities, and therefore it may be difficult nowadays
to determine with certainty, from which opus among
his instrumental works, known to us now mostly by
their titles only, J. S. Bach made his selection for the
current arrangements."

1867

The essay of Julius Rühlmann "Antonio Vivaldi and his influence on J. S. Bach" appears in the "Neue Zeitschrift für Musik." He calls Vivaldi's works "nearly completely missing."

1905

In the "Geschichte des Instrumentalkonzerts" (History of the Instrumental Concerto) by Arnold Schering, Vivaldi is dealt with on 19 pages. Schering calls him "one of the most progressive musicians and one of the most talented minds of the century."

1906

Suddenly, Vivaldi's name is the center of interest with public and critics alike, as Fritz Kreisler performs a violin concerto of his own under the name of Vivaldi. It was printed in New York in 1927, and practically all great soloists included it in their repertoire. (Kreisler admitted authorship only in 1935.)

1909

The Englishman Alfred Muffat starts publication of four works by Vivaldi at Schott.

1912

The Hungarian violinist Tivador Nachèz publishes in Edition Schott six works by Vivaldi; in years to come, twelve others follow.

April 1922

The "Thematic Catalogue of the printed works of Antonio Vivaldi, along with a listing of new editions and arrangements" by Wilhelm Altmann is published. (Allgemeine Musikalische Zeitung, pp. 262–279)

1926–1932

At the Collegio San Carlo near San Martino (Province of Alessandria in Upper Italy), a collection of musical manuscripts in 97 volumes is found, among them 14 volumes containing works of Vivaldi. Thanks to the special efforts made by Alberto Gentili, it is safeguarded in the Biblioteca Nazionale in Turin. The collections Mauro Foà and Renzo Giordano are founded. The first performances from them under the direction of A. Gentili take place in Turin on January 28, 1928.

Ill. 6: Poster on the occasion of the Vivaldi Week in Siena, 1939

1939

Alfredo Casella writes in the programm notes for the Settimana Vivaldiana 1939 in Siena:
"The first consideration was to show all aspects of the gigantic figure of the 'preto rosso,' the dramatic stage music, the sacred and the instrumental music including the chamber music."

1947

Marc Pincherle's standard work "Antonio Vivaldi et la musique instrumentale" with an "Inventaire thématique" is published.

c. 1965

In an interview, a French bicycle racer was asked, if he liked music.
"Very much, especially Vivaldi."
"Why?"
"Because he has formidable sprints from time to time."
(He probably meant the Ritornello and its recurrence!)

Ill. 7: Italian stamp honoring Vivaldi, 1975

1972—1975

In the record catalogues of these years, over 50 recordings of the Concertos, Op. 8 Nos. 1 to 4 ("The Seasons") are listed. How resistant these works are to arrangements, is shown by the recording Angel S-37450. On it, "The Seasons" are played by the Tokyo New Koto Ensemble (6 kotos) under the direction of Seiji Mitsuishi, with Tomoko Sunazaki as soloist. Minoru writes on the record jacket:

"The purists may call it blasphemy. Some "progressive" musicians and musicologists may treat this event with a scornful eye as a superficial effort to have "the East meet the West." No matter what conclusion one draws, it cannot be denied that a different new world exists now for Vivaldi."

Ill. 8 b

Ill. 8 a

Ill. 8 a/b: Medal struck on the tercentenary of the birth of Antonio Vivaldi by the Monnaie de Paris. Obverse and reverse

1978

"In the Largo of the "Winter" Concerto, Vivaldi proves his unusual sensitivity toward the cosmic rhythm of the seasons."

(Jean-Louis Degaudenzi in a review of the record "Airs et Adagios baroques, Invitation à la Musique," Philips 6833 196, in: Nostra, Magazine, l'hebdomadaire de l' actualité mystérieuse, 11—17 janvier 1978)

Life and works
Youth

". . . that music has its true place
in this city." (p. 260)
(Francesco Sansovino, Venetia
città nobilissima e singolare . . .
1581, ampliata da Giovanni Strin-
ga, Venetia 1604)

In 1963, the German-English Emil Paul worked in the
Venetian archives on the history of the violin. After
finishing his research, he had a little time left and got the
idea to check if it were perhaps possible to find out the
birth date of Vivaldi. After a few minutes he held in his
hands the document which so many musicologists had
been looking for for decades and for which the archives
of the entire diocese of Venice had been minutely examined on an official basis. All assumptions about "the blood
of courageous seafarers which (supposedly) ran through
his veins" and which fitted so nicely the liveliness of his
music, were worthless. The fact is that in 1291 two brothers named Vivaldi tried to find the sea route to India and
perished near the Canary Islands!

The family Vivaldi originated in Brescia where the grand-
parents Agostin and Margherita lived as middle-class
house owners. The father of the composer, Giovanni
Battista, was born in Brescia in 1655. He went to Venice
with his mother at the age of ten, learned the barber's
trade and kept busy in his spare time as a violinist. The
combination barber/musician occurred often in the Italy
of the 17th and 18th centuries, since instruments used to
hang on the walls of barber shops and were played by the
waiting customers to kill time, perhaps also by the barbers
themselves when they waited for customers.

19

Ill. 9: Document of June 6, 1676, showing that Giovan Battista Vivaldi and Camilla Calicchio were unmarried (Registro di stato libero, Parrocchia di San Giovanni in Bràgora, Venezia)

On August 6, 1676, he married Camilla Calicchio, the daughter of a tailor, in Venice and on March· 4, 1678 Antonio was born. Because of his frail health, he had an emergency christening by the midwife; the regular baptism took place in the church of San Giovanni in Bràgora. The document reads:

"On May 6, 1678
Antonio Lucio, son of Signor Gio. Battista, [son] of the late Agustin Vivaldi, musician, and of Camilla, daughter of the late Camillo Calicchio, his wife, born on March 4 of this year and christened because of mortal danger by the godmother and widwife Margarita Veronese, was brought to the church today and received baptism from me, Giacomo Panacieri Piovano. Signor Antonio, son of the late Vecchio, apothecary at the sign of the Doge, in this quarter, was godfather."

(Venice, Church of San Giovanni in Bràgora, parish register)

Ill. 10: Certificate of baptism of Vivaldi (Venice, Church of San Giovanni in Bràgora, Libro de' Battesimi)

Since the father is called "sonador" (musician, instrumentalist) in the certificate of baptism, he seems to have made a complete change-over to the musical profession by this time. By the way, Antonio had four brothers, some of whom will be mentioned later on, as well as two sisters. All of them apparently had never practised music actively, but two nephews were professionally employed as music copyists: Pietro Mauro, the son of Vivaldi's sister Cecilia Maria, and Carlo, the son of his brother Francesco Gaetano.

Ill. 11: Venezia. Map of Venice, bird's eye view. Engraving from the 17th century.

When Antonio was seven years old, his father progressed further in his career, and this change was to have considerable consequences for the musical development of the boy. In 1685, a "Sovvegno de musicisti di Santa Cecilia" was founded in Venice, a kind of social insurance institution on a religious basis, and Vivaldi's father was one of the founding members. The assistant conductor of San Marco, Giovanni Legrenzi, was selected as chairman of this society. When he was nominated during the same year as Primo Maestro at the cathedral, his first measure in the reorganization of church music was an enlargement of the orchestra to 34 members consisting of:

8 violini	2 viole da gamba	2 cornetti
11 violette	1 violone	1 fagotto
2 viole da braccio	4 tiorbe	3 tromboni.

Ill. 12: Francesco Guardi (1712−1793): Piazza San Marco

Vivaldi's father was one of the newly hired members as the council decision shows:

On April 23, 1685

The undersigned Hon. representatives, consisting of Gio. Battista Cornaro, Marco Ruzini, Giulio Giustinian, Alvise Mocenigo IV., Silvestro Valier, Ottaviano Marini, Zaccaria Vallaresso, Francesco Cornaro have, in the absence of the Hon. representative Giovanni Pisano, decided that in the capella of the Doge's Church of San Marco the men mentioned below will be accepted for the concerts with the usual payment of 15 ducats for each of them, and that they will be entered in the "Libro de conformità" immediately, in order that they can take part on similar occasions, their names being:

23

Ill. 13: Giovanni Antonio Canal, called Canaletto (1697–1768): Venice, Piazzetta San Marco

Francesco Valletta, Viola da Braccio, with 15 ducats, Gio. Baptista Rossi, Violin, with 15 ducats,
Lodovico Vaccio, Trombone, with 15 ducats.
  Yes votes 7
  No votes —
  Abstentions 1
(Archive of the State, Venice, Procuratori . . . San Marco, Reg. 148, Orders and Resolutions c. 59t)

The document is especially interesting, because Vivaldi's father is called Gio. Baptista Rossi; the sandy hair color being conspicuous in Italy, he was apparently better known by it than by his real name, and we will see this fact repeated in the case of his son.

His father's joining the famous orchestra of San Marco was of far-reaching importance to the young Vivaldi, since he was now brought into contact with the milieu of this illustrious musical group. It can be assumed that he was allowed to listen at an early age to rehearsals and performances and grew up to an understanding of the music played, especially the works of Legrenzi.

We are informed about his musical education solely through unreliable sources. He may very well have studied the violin with his father; the fact that he was also a student of theory with Legrenzi, is doubted by some authors (while others maintain the truth of it), since Legrenzi died soon thereafter on May 27, 1690. If one takes Antonio's early maturity for granted — he belonged clearly to the type of masters creating at an early age and without effort —, there is no reason to doubt his having been Legrenzi's pupil. A "Laetatus" dated 1691 which is preserved in Turin in a copy without the name of the author, may quite possibly have resulted from such lessons.

The father was also active as a pedagogue; a notice exists in the documents at the Ospedale dei Mendicanti, dated July 22,1689:

"Election of Gio. Batta Vivaldi detto Rosetto as instrumental teacher."
(Rubriche dell'ospedale dei Mendicanti)

At the age of ten, Antonio is said to have played in the orchestra of San Marco, occasionally substituting for his father who often played in the theatre orchestra of San Giovanni Grisostomo. Other sources indicate his becoming in his younger years a member of the cathedral orchestra, but no proof for this assertion exists. The salary account book of the cathedral shows Giovanni Battista Vivaldi as a musician who enjoyed a growing esteem: in 1689, his salary was raised to 25 ducats.

We are better informed about Antonio from the time, when he received the tonsure on September 18, 1693 at the age of 15 1/2 years and on the following day became "ostiario," reaching the first of the four minor orders. In the documents referring to his priestly education, he is sometimes called a member of the parish of San Geminiani, also of San Giovanni in Oleo, but no seminary of priests is ever mentioned. In those days, it was actually possible to become a priest without joining such a seminary, simply by being, in a manner of speaking, assigned to a parish priest as apprentice and assistant.

He may have preferred this career, since this somewhat loose connection outside an institution left him relatively much time for his musical studies. The ultimate decision to choose priesthood may have been made on the basis of the Italian custom during the 17th and 18th century which permitted quite definitely the simultaneous pursuit of the profession of a musician and the life of a priest.

Ill. 14 a/b: Documents related to the religious career of Vivaldi. Venice, Archivio Patriciarcale, Registro Sacre Ordinazioni 1688—1706

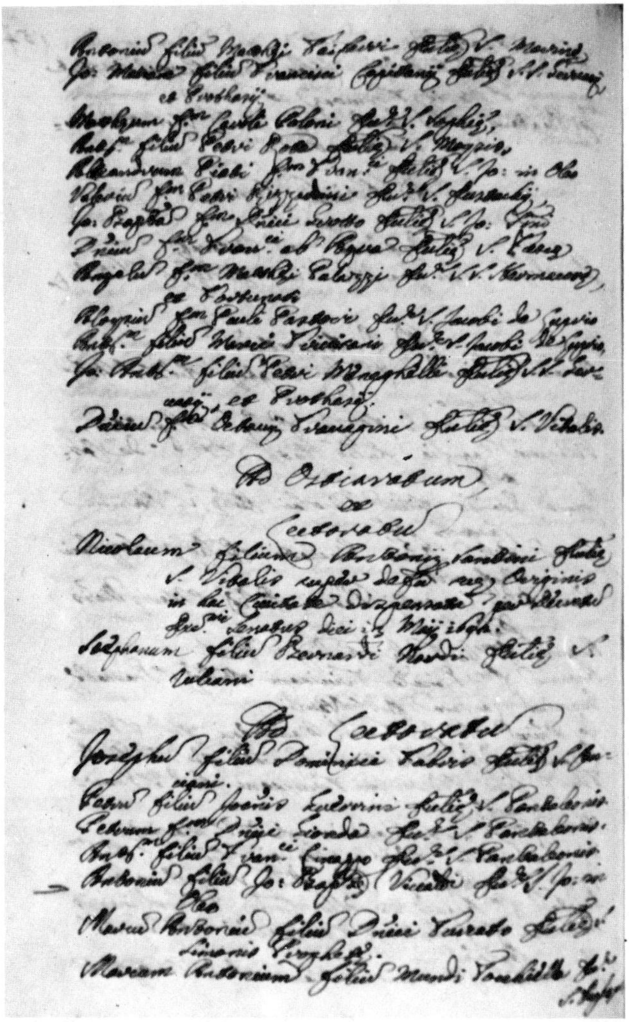
Ad Ostiariatum et Lectoratum

Ad Lectoratum

Ill. 14 c

Ill. 14 d

Ill. 14 e

Ill. 14 f

32

Ill. 14 b

The first document dealing with his career as a priest reads:

"On Friday, September 18, 1693, in the chapel of the palace of the Patriarch of Venice, the Hon. Reverend D. D. Johannes Baduarius, by God's mercy Patriarch of Venice and Dalmatia

Ill. 14 g

and Prince of the Church, marked the following with the tonsure: Antonio, son of Giovanni Battista Vivaldi from the parish of San Geminiani . . .

The entries for the four minor and the three higher orders read similarly; Vivaldi became:

    Ostiario on September 19, 1693
    Lettore on September 21, 1694
    Esorcista on December 25, 1695
    Accolita on September 21, 1696

             *

    Suddiacono on April 4, 1699
    Diacono on September 18, 1700
    Sacerdote on March 24, 1703

Ill. 15: Venice, Palazzo Ducale, Sala del Maggior Consiglio

The violin teacher

Growing fame as an instrumental composer

Once Vivaldi was consecrated as a priest on March 24, 1703, the events of the following years suggest that he felt more like a professional musician than a clergyman right from the beginning. In September of the same year, he already had become violin teacher at the Seminario dell'Ospedale della Pietà, and the cashbooks contain the record indicating an initial payment on March 17, 1704 of the amount of 30 ducats covering the past semester, i.e., five ducats for each month.

> *"D. Antonio Vivaldi, Maestro di Choro, must be given 30 ducats as payment for six months which ended this past February."*

This was an new position specially created by Gasparini. The council order of August 12, 1703 reads:

"New teachers for the Chorus.

"To continue perfecting the ensemble and give it a greater purity of sound, as proposed by Signor Gasparini, our Maestro di Choro, it is necessary that our representatives for the chorus select teachers for viola, violin and oboe, to be given a remuneration which they consider appropriate and which is of the least burden to the institution. They are to be kept in service for as long as it appears necessary, and it remains stipulated what they and the institution are to accomplish."

The son made rapid progress, as his father had done before him, and in August his salary was already raised by 40 ducats a year, when he added the title of Maestro da Viola all'Inglese (whereby the viola and violetta are probably understood, since the term never appeared in the employment listings).

Ill. 16: Vincenzo Coronelli (died 1718): Veduta della Riva degli Schiavoni con la regatta. The second building from the left was the place of activity of Vivaldi. The Chiesa della Pietà o della Visitazione which stands there now is the work of Giorgio Massari (1745) and was consecrated in 1760.

The document reads:

"Today's date August 17, 1704

"Since Don Antonio Vivaldi continues as violin teacher of the girls and with industrious presence also with the lessons on the viola inglese which, however, is considered by his superiors as being beyond his regular employment, it has been decided that a further 40 ducats a year is added to his customary salary for teaching the viola inglese, so that he is encouraged in his work by a total of 100 ducats a year. This also to the further benefit of the girls."

9 Yes votes

accepted

1 No vote

The type of institution where Vivaldi taught was called in the older literature, not very aptly, a conservatory, and he himself sometimes even the director of the conservatory. This asks for a correction. In a port city of the size and importance of Venice, which was for decades involved in wars, especially with the Turks, there were orphans, illegitimate children, foundlings in large number, and to take care of them, orphanages were founded quite early which were affiliated with hospitals for better care of the wards; therefore the name *"Ospedale."* The oldest was founded by Frate Pietruccio di Assisi as early as 1346. Since these Venetian institutions accommodated at times up to 6000 youths, the public resources were not nearly sufficient to support them, and therefore donations from the public and endowments were depended upon. In the general teaching and educational schedule, choral singing was encouraged considerably, since it served the organization of religious services. These choral classes developed in four of these orphanages into music seminaries for the specially talented wards; these were La Pietà, I Mendicanti, Gli Incurabili and L'Ospedaletto, all four of whom accommodated girls exclusively. Famous maestri were engaged as teachers; Caldara, Galuppi, Hasse, Legrenzi, Lotti, Domenico Scarlatti, Tessarini, Traetta and others were teaching at these institutions. La Pietà was specializing in instrumental music, and this is where the exceptional violinist Vivaldi found a sphere of activity entirely to his liking. The regular Sunday and holiday concerts were gala events in the musical life of the city; they were attended regularly; the accomplishments of the girl soloists were compared; and the young Venetian gentlemen preferred to pick their future wives from among the girls playing and singing there.

The management of the institutions furthered these concerts actively, since the income from renting seats contributed in considerable measure to their income.

Ill. 17: Francesco Guardi (1712–1793): Venice, Riva degli Schiavoni. Partly obscured by the sail: Chiesa della Pietà

Various actions indicate how clearly the interest in good results was furthered. In 1688, as an example, it was decided that one third of the money collected at the church services belonged to the director, the balance being divided, after deducting the fees for sacristan and teacher, between chorus and orchestra. Two years later, the salary of the director was raised considerably, and the entire money collected belonged to the participating girls. These were, incidentally, invisible; a heavy grille hid them from the glances of the curious.

No traveler to Italy, from the Russian Petr Andreevitch Toltago in 1698 up to Goethe in 1790, missed this unique opportunity to hear the best music in such captivating and at the same time mysterious circumstances. The former reported to Russia:

"There are nunneries in Venice whose inhabitants play the organ and other instruments and sing so beautifully that one will look in vain anywhere in the world for such sweet and harmonious singing. That is the reason for people coming to Venice from all over the world, desiring to take in these angelic voices, especially those in the convent of the incurables."

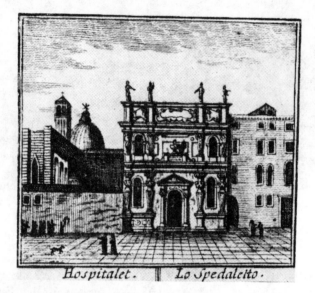

Hospitalet. || Lo Spedaletto.

Ill. 18: Luca Carlevarijs (1703): Facciata della Chiesa dell' Ospedale dei Derelitti, called Ospedaletto

Others compared the accomplishments, especially at La Pietà, with the orchestra of the Paris Opéra, and the latter by no means always was preferred. Charles de Brosses who traveled through Italy from June 1739 to April 1740 addressed letters to his friends containing enthusiastic descriptions of music life in Venice. He wrote to Monsieur de Blancey on August 29, 1739:

40

*Ill. 19: Giovanni Antonio Canal, called Canaletto
(1697–1768): Venice, Dogana and Riva delle Zattere*

*Ill. 20: Canaletto (1697–1768): Venice, Il Rio
dei Mendicanti*

Ill. 21: Francesco Guardi (1712—1793): Gala concert in honor of Grand Duke Paul and Grand Duchess Maria Feodorovna in the Sala dei Filarmonici in Venice, 1782

"The most exquisite music here is that of the Ospedali. There are four of them, all occupied by illegitimate girls or those whose parents are incapable of bringing them up. They are educated at the expense of the state, and they are trained solely with the purpose of excelling in music. That is why they sing like angels and play violin, flute, organ, oboe, cello, bassoon; in short, no instrument is so big as to frighten them. They are kept like nuns in a convent. All they do is perform concerts, always in groups of about forty girls. I swear to you that there is nothing as pleasant as seeing a young and pretty nun, dressed in white, with a little pomegranate bouquet over her ears, conducting the orchestra with all the gracefulness and incredible precision one can imagine. Their voices are beautifully controlled and light, because one does not know here what round tones and spun-out notes à la française are. La Zabaleta at the Incurabili is most astonishing because of her range and the technique she has in her throat. I do not doubt that she has swallowed the violin of Somis. She receives stormy applause, and if anybody compared her to another singer, the people would beat him half-dead. But listen, my friends, I believe that nobody is listening to us, and so I whisper into your ears that Margarita of the Mendicanti is just as good and I like her even better.

"The one of the four Ospedali I visit most often and like best, is La Pietà; it is also the foremost because of the perfection of the orchestra. What precision of performance! Only here does one hear those superb ways of bowing which are admired, without justification, at the Paris Opéra. La Chiaretta would surely be the supreme violinist in Italy, if Anna-Maria of the Ospedaletto did not surpass her by far."

Incidentally, the girls were divided into two groups, "di comun," i.e., the musically less talented ones, and "di coro," who could be used in chorus and orchestra. It was a nice custom that they were called after their instrument instead of their surname — which most of them did not have —: Michieletta del violino, Lucieta dalla viola, Geltruda dalla violetta, Cattarina del cornetto, Luciana organista, etc. The public talked, for example, of Marietta della Pietà who also performed in operas.

Vivaldi who was at first only teaching the violin, soon found a wider field of activity, since the then director of the music class, Francesco Gasparini, a good composer and author of a thoroughbass method which was reprinted several times, absented himself often in opera matters and also was frequently ill. It is documented that he soon assumed also the function of Maestro del Coro (director of the ensemble) and of Maestro de'Concerti (director of performances) and enriched the repertoire by adding works of his own:

"June 2, 1715

"*The institution acknowledges from the request of the Rev. Antonio Vivaldi, violin teacher in the orchestra of the institution, and from the previously read document of the directors of our administration of the ensemble the well-known diligence and the successful efforts on his part, not only regarding the success and general satisfaction in educating the girls in instrumental concerts, but also through excellent compositions which he contributed during the absence of the above-mentioned Maestro Gasparini, an entire mass, a vesper, an oratorio, more than 30 motets and other works. In order to give just recognition, prove its gratitude and acknowledge such extraordinary efforts at least partially, it has been voted to pay him this time from our cash office 50 ducats because of our pleasure in his eagerness and his extra-ordinary efforts. They are to serve also as a lively encourage-ment to contribute more and more to the perfection of the girls in our ensemble which is so necessary for the ensemble it-self and for the greater glory of this our church.*"

With the five sixths
   Abstentions —
   No votes 2
   Yes votes 10

The growing fame of the orchestra of La Pietà was cer-tainly due in great measure to Vivaldi's work.

An event which imaginative biographers seized on fre-quently happened during the period when his obligations multiplied constantly: Vivaldi freed himself from parts of

Ill. 22: Giovanni Battista Brustolon (1712–1796): The Bucintoro, the Venetian ship of state. Engraving after Canaletto (1697–1768)

his clerical duties by not celebrating mass any longer. He suffered occasionally from angina pectoris, apparently an inherited ailment, so that he had to leave the altar several times. Dispensation from reading mass was without doubt granted by his church superiors due to the condition of his health, but it is asserted that he went to the vestry several times during the mass, in order to write down themes which suddenly occurred to him. The next step in letting imagination of these biographers run wild was that he fell into the hands of the inquisition, and in our own times Franz Farga insisted even that Vivaldi "took off the priestly garments, in order to dedicate himself entirely to music." A certain Fantoni, however, gave his imagination the fullest rein by considering the singer Anna Giraud the "legitimate wife" of Vivaldi.

Fortunately, the maestro himself has spoken up on this matter in a letter of November 16, 1737 to the Marchese Guido Bentivoglio d'Aragona:

"It is now 25 years, since I last read a mass, and I do not want to do so again, not by prohibition or order, as you can let His Eminence know, but of my own accord because of an illness which I have suffered from the day of my birth and which affects me considerably.

"As soon as I was ordained as a priest, I read mass for a little over a year and gave it up, since I had to leave the altar three times without finishing mass, because I felt ill.. That is the reason why I spend most of my life at home or leave only in a gondola or a carriage, since I cannot walk due to my respiratory ailment, also called difficulty in breathing.

"No nobleman invites me, not even our doge, since they all know of my illness. Immediately after my midday meal, I can usually leave the house, but never on foot. This is the reason why I do not celebrate mass."

An unexplained question remains: if Vivaldi could not hold out during an entire mass, how was he possibly equal to the much heavier strain of a traveling virtuoso, the excitement of an opera impresario, the drudgery and daily routine with its deadlines of an opera composer of the 18th century? Why did Vivaldi not resume reading mass later on, when his health was presumably improved somewhat? All these questions could, of course, only have been answered by him alone. It is true that the church lost a good reader of the mass, but the world of music, on the other hand, gained a larger number of concertos and quite a few operas. The conflict between the assumed obligations and the growing musical appointments was probably not easy for him to bear; let us hope that all his beautiful church compositions will be credited and balanced against the unfulfilled priestly obligations. . .

A personal conjecture regarding Vivaldi's problematic priesthood may find a place here: it is known through the research of Giazotto that Venice suffered a heavy earthquake on the day of Vivaldi's birth which laid sections of the city in ruins. There is a chance that the premature birth can be attributed to this event. Perhaps the frightened mother promised to dedicate her oldest son to the priesthood, if he remained alive; Antonio accepted the obligation in any case, but suffered from it, as his activities as a musician continued to expand. That made his dispensation from reading mass convenient for him, and his conduct of life was the result of this development. But we know from several sources, especially from the meeting with Goldoni, that he was very religious and retained his habit of reading prayers from his breviary even when his opera compositions kept him very busy.

In 1711, Vivaldi's Opus III, his famous 12 Concertos "L'Estro Armonico," was published by Roger in Amsterdam, and this editor was to distribute his works all over the civilized world, as it existed in those times, in future years. The published works are:

(Op. III) L'Estro Armonico (The Harmonic Inspiration) Concerti/Consacrati/All'Altezza Reale/Di/Ferdinando III/Gran Principe di Toscana/da D. Antonio Vivaldi/Musico di Violino e Maestro de Concerti/del/pio Ospidale della Pietà di Venezia/ Opera Terza/A Amsterdam/Aux dépens d'Estienne Roger Marchand Libraire N^O 50/51 (Reprinted by Le Clerc le Cadet in Paris and by J. Walsh and J. Hare, London.). Published in 1711.

(Op. IV) La Stravaganze (The Extravagance) (12) Concerti/Consacrati a Sua Eccellenza/Il Sig. Vettor Delfino/Nobile Veneto/ da/D. Antonio Vivaldi/Musico di Violino, e Maestro de Concerti/ del Pio Ospitale della Pietà di Venetia/Opera Quarta/ A Amsterdam/Chez Estienne Roger Marchand Libraire/N^O 399/400 (reprinted by J. Walsh and J. Hare, London.). Published c. 1712.

(Op. V) VI Sonate/Quatro a Violino Solo e Basso/e due/a due Violini e Basso Continuo/di Antonio Vivaldi/Opera Quinta/ O Vero Parte Seconda del Opera Seconda/A Amsterdam /chez Jeanne Roger n.^{O} 418. Published c. 1716.

(Op. VI) VI Concerti/à Cinque Stromenti, tre Violini, Alto Viola e Basso Continuo/di D. Antonio Vivaldi/Musico di Violino, e Maestro de Concerti/del Pio Ospitale della Pietà di Venetia/ Opera Sesta/A Amsterdam/Chez Jeanne Roger/N^O 452. Published c. 1716/1717.

(Op. VII) (12) Concerti/à Cinque Stromenti, tre Violini/Alto Viola e Basso Continuo/di D. Antonio Vivaldi/Musico di Violino, e Maestro de Concerti/del Pio Ospidale della Pietà di Venetia/ Opera Settima. Uno è con Oboe./A. Amsterdam/chez Jeanne Roger/N^O 470—471. Published c. 1716/1717.

(Op. VIII) Il Cimento dell'Armonia/e dell'Inventione (The Venture of Harmony and Invention)/(12) Concerti/ a 4 e 5/ Consacrati/All'Illustrissimo Signore/Il Signor Venceslao Conte di Marzin, Signore Ereditario/di Hohenelbe, Lomnitz, Tschista, Krzinetz, Kaunitz, Doubek,/et Sowoluska, Cameriere Attuale, e Consigliere di/S.M.C.C./Da D. Antonio Vivaldi/Maestro in Italia dell'Illustrissimo Signor Conte Sudetto,/Maestro dè Concerti del Pio Ospitale della Pietà in Venetia,/e Maestro di Capella di S.A.S. il Signor/Principe Filippo Langravio d'Hassia Darmithath./Opera Ottava/A Amsterdam/Spesa di Michele Carlo Le Cene/Libraro/N^O 520—521. (Reprint by Le Clerc le Cadet, Paris.) Published 1725.

(Op. IX) La Cetra (The Lyra)/(12) Concerti/Consacrati/Alla/ Sacra, Cesarea, Cattolica, Real Maesta/di/Carlo VI/Imperadore/ e Terzo Re delle Spagne/di Bohemia di Ungaria, etc, etc, etc./ da D. Antonio Vivaldi/Musico di Violino, Maestro de Pio Ospitale/della Gittà di Venetia e Maestro di Capella/di Camera di S.A.S. Il Sig^r Principe Filippo Langravio d'Hassia Darmstaht/ Opera Nona/A Amsterdam/Spesa di Michéle Carlo Le Cene/ Libraire/n^O 533—534. Published in 1728.

(Op. X) VI Concerti/a Flauto Traverso/Violino Primo e Secondo Alto Viola/Organo e Violoncello/DDi/D. Antonio Vivaldi/Musico di Violino, Maestro del Pio Ospitale/della Citta di Venetia e Maestro di Capella/di Camera di S.A.S. Il Sig^r Il Principe/Filippo Langravio d'Hassia Darmistaht/Opera Decima/Amsterdam/a Spesa di Michele Carlo Le Cene N^O 544. Published c. 1728.

(Op. XI) Sei/Concerti/a Violino Principale, Violino Primo e Secondo/Alto Viola, Organo e Violoncello/di/D. Antonio Vivaldi/

Ill. 23: Canaletto (1697—1768): Venice, La Scala dei Giganti, Palazzo Ducale

Musico di Violino, Maestro del Pio Ospitale della Citta di Venetia e Maestro di Capella/di Camera di S.A.S. Il Sig[r] Principe/Filippo Langravio d'Hassia Darmstadt/Opera Undecima/Amsterdam/A Spesa di Michele Carlo Le Cene/N[o] 545. Published in 1729.

(Op. XII) Sei/Concerti/a Violino Principale, Violino Primo e Secondo/Alto Viola, Organo e Violoncello/di D. Antonio Vivaldi/Musico di Violino, Maestro del Pio Ospitale della Citta di Venetia e Maestro di Capella/di Camera di S.A.S. Il Sig[r] Principe/Filippo Langravio d'Hassia Darmstadt/Opera duodecima/Amsterdam/a Spesa di Michele Carlo Le Cene./N° 546. Published in 1729.

(Op. XIII) Il Pastor Fido,/Sonates,/pour la Muzette, Viele, Flûte, Hautbois, Violon/avec le Basse Continüe/Del Sig[r]/ Antonio Vivaldi./Opera XIII[a]./prix en blanc 6.[tt]/A Paris/chez Me Boivin M[de] rue St Honoré à la Règle d'or./Avec Privilège du Roy. Published c. 1737.

(Op. XIV?) VI Sonates/Violoncelle Solo/col Basso/da Antonio Vivaldi/Musico di Violino è Maestro dé Concerti/del Pio Ospidale della Pietà di Venezia/gravé par Mlle Michelon/Prix 5[tt]/ A Paris/chez M[r] le Clerc le cadet rue S[t] Honoré à la ville de Constantinople près l'Oratoire/M[r] le Clerc M[d] rue du Roule a la Croix d'Or,/Mme Boivin M[de] rue S[t] Honoré à la Règle d'Or./ Avec Privilège du Roy. Published c. 1740.

Estienne Roger, the active French emigrant — his family was forced to leave their native country because of the revocation of the Edict of Nantes —, had become within a relatively short period of time the leading music publisher in Europe. A modern music printing technique developed especially for use in instrumental music, in which the groups metrically belonging together are combined by common crossbars, as in these examples:

made the editions of Roger superior to his competitors who were still using the old vocal notation. He was the inventor of the edition numbers which simplified matters in advertising and ordering. They were used in the past only to keep the printing blocks in good order. (In the beginning, the blocks of works where a reprint did not pay were removed and the released numbers were assigned to new works. This accounts for some wrong dating of works by Vivaldi according to their edition numbers!) But Roger also had an instinct for talents, and so he added Vivaldi who was geographically far removed, to the circle of his authors.

In the preface to his opus III, the composer says:

"To the music lovers,
"The courteous consideration you have extended to my efforts
up to now, made me try to give pleasure also with an instrumental
concerto. I freely admit that, since my compositions previously
had, in addition to their faults, also the disadvantage of their
printing, there is now the great improvement to have them
engraved by the famous hand of Monsieur Estienne Roger.
This is the reason for my endeavor to satisfy you with the print-
ing of these concertos, and it encourages me also to submit soon
another series of concertos a 4. Please preserve me your favor and
live happily."

The sentence mentioning that in the past his works had suffered from poor printing, is especially interesting. In 1705, the trio sonatas, Op. I were published by the editor Giuseppe Sala, in 1708/9 the violin sonatas, Op. II by Antonio Bortoli, both in Venice.

(Op. I) Suonate da Camera/a tre/Due Violini e Violone o Cembalo/di/D. Antonio Vivaldi/Musico di Violino, Professore Veneto/Opera Prima . . .

(Op. II) Sonate/A Violino, e Basso per il Cembalo/Consagrate/ A Sua Maesta/Il Re/Federico/Quarto/DI Danimarka, e Norvegia, Duca di Slesvig, di Olstein, di Stormar e di Ditmarsia,/ Conte di Oldemburgo, di Del-/menorst, ec, ec, ec./Da D. Antonio Vivaldi/Musico di Violino, e Maestro de' Concerto del Pio Ospidale/della Pietà di Venezia/ . . .

At this point, a basic remark must be made about the printed works of Vivaldi: according to the custom of those times, 12 or 6 works having the same instrumentation were usually combined in one printing. In the literature one often finds sentences like "Already in 1709, Vivaldi had . . ." or "Only in 1729 . . ." These statements are based on the erroneous assumption that the composer had written the works in question one after another during or shortly before the year of publication. In reality, works published together were written years, even decades apart; if an offer was made by a publisher, the composer looked in his drawer and, if time permitted, wrote a few more works to complete the set, made a few adjustments and sent the collection off. To establish the correct chronology, the dates of printed works can, therefore, only be used with utmost caution. Quite a few compositions which were handed down to us through manuscripts in Turin, prove this custom.

In his Opus I, Vivaldi calls himself simply "Musico di Violino, Professore Veneto;" in Opus II, he is already "Maestro d'Concerti del Pio Ospedale della Pietà di Venezia." Vivaldi's reputation for his instrument is based on Opus I, some of whose sonatas are sure to have been known in Venice before 1705. While as early as in the beginning of the 17th century a budding composer proved himself as a maestro through a collection of madrigals (Monteverdi, Henricus Sagittarius, et al.), now, at the height of popularity of instrumental music, a dozen trio sonatas were presented by the composer, like a musical calling card, to the world of music and especially to his colleagues. We can assume that several works from this collection had a definite influence on his appointment at the Ospedale.

*Ill. 24: Page 19 of the Italian edition of the violin sonatas,
Op. II, Venice 1709, at Antonio Bortoli*

Since Vivaldi, much like Corelli in his Opus V, put variations on "La Folia" at the end, and also for several thematic suggestions, a direct relationship as a pupil of the Roman master has been inferred on the strength of Opus I, all the more so since there was an unusually long interval of four years between the "suddiacono" and the ordination. But no documentary evidence for this suggestion exists. The influence of Corelli may simply be due to Vivaldi's knowledge of his music, because the trio sonatas had been available in print since 1681 and the Opus V in 1700, incidentally both reprinted in Venice in 1701 and 1705 respectively. It can be taken for granted that Vivaldi had known and played them.

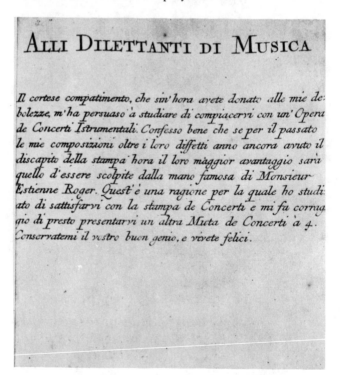

Ill. 25: Preface "To the Music Lovers" to Op. III

It is more important than finding reminiscences of Corelli — both included typical melodic formulas of their times in their musical vocabulary — to compare the structure of their trio sonatas. This results in the fact that Corelli used a type of canzona relatively simple in melodic and technical form, while in Vivaldi a higher degree of development in combinations presents itself. Fugatos appear frequently, also exchanges of voices, motivic relation between movements, variants of formally related parts, assimilated sections of themes, etc. All this indicates intensive studies and a well-practised ease of writing. Opus I must have been preceded by a full production of compositions in his youth, which Vivaldi may have considered as practice pieces and therefore have suppressed.

The sonatas, Opus II were probably written in part for his own use, in part surely as exercises for his girl students. This is suggested often by the constant use of eighths, triplets, sixteenths appearing in the gigues and other movements where a technical problem is treated. A century prior to the invention of the violin etudes, this gave students a chance to comprehend technical problems in playing the instrument. Examples are the movements named Capriccio in the sonatas No. 9 and 12, the Fantasia of the No. 11 or the Corrente in No. 8.

The sonatas, opus II are mainly known in a printed edition which in 1709 was given a dedication to Frederic IV. of Denmark and Norway who visited Venice on Saturday, December 29, 1708 with a retinue of 50 persons and was asked by the town clerk about his wishes. The answer was: for the same evening a loge in the Teatro San Giovanni Grisostomo, for the next one a concert at the Pietà, for Monday a visit of the city in a "banta" (a masked gown). Vivaldi conducted the concert "in assenza (absence) del Gasparini."

Ill. 26: Francesco Guardi (1712–1793): Venice, Veduta del Canale Grande vista dal Rialto

The dedication suggests some personal contact; it is the first document of its kind which survives of Vivaldi, and it is written in the style of the most devout submission customary in those times.

"Your Majesty,

"The fate of the devoted heart is to be envied when it is forced, in meeting a monarch great by birth and even greater by his mental gifts, to be certain that his accomplishments are well received. This truth which forces my mind to admire the heroic spirit, well-known everywhere, of Your Majesty, makes me fully confident in offering my modest works which could not be reduced in any way through properly thinking of me as a nonen-

tity. Your fate would not have made you greater and put you on an elevated place, noticeable by the majesty and by the power; but your greatness was of so little use, because it was too far removed from those who are deep down. You have stepped down from your throne, and the submissiveness surmounted the obstacles of Your Highness, in order to console him who knows himself, bent down, to be unworthy to kiss even the bottom step of your throne. Please acknowledge, o great King, not the offered work which has no relation to your person, but the heart offering it, since only the heart can be of value to something that has none,

ALTEZZA REALE

Potrebbe forse riuscire di poco applauso a chi dal suo forma giudizio d'un animo veramente regio, quest'opera, quale con tutto l'essequio del cuore umilio al merito sopraggrande di V.A.R. perche troppo sproportionata ella sia alla Vostra Venerata Grandezza. Havrei 'n fatti sottoscritto ancor io ad un tale malfondato parere, se non mi fossi corretto nel riflettere, che quest'è una dici: amla, sfortuna a cui soggiaccione e'l Prencipe, perche non puo essere riconosciuto, com'egli merita e'l popolo, perche non puo offerire, com'esso deve: onde in Quello il compatimento deve uguagliar alla sua Altezza ciò che appena può stargli a piedi; ed in questo deve supplire un gran cuore a diffetti necessary della sua conditione. Sia dunque per esser qual si voglia questo picciol tributo della mia umilissima divozione, lascia egli d'esser ciò, che in vero egl'è, mentre e so, che voi avete riguardo n'à ciò, che vi si offerisce, mà alla sincera umilità di chi vi offerisce, e posso aver una ferma confidenza nella somma Benignità del Vostro Animo Eccelso, che niente sdegna, e tutto accoglie. Questa verità, siccome liberera me da Critici disinganando la riverenza loro troppo indiscretta; mi dà altresì del coraggio non ordinario per comparirvi tutto sommesso dinanzi al Soglio e protestar con quest'atto esterno di soggezione l'inalterabil rispetto dell'animo che solo mi fu stimolo, perche inventassi maniere di darne al publico una viva testimonianza, con cui per sempre mi consagro.

Umiliss. Devotiss. et
Ossequiosiss. Servitore
ANTONIO VIVALDI.

Ill. 27: Dedication of Op. III to the Grand Duke of Tuscany

and weight where there is none. You should not avert your eye
from this simple present because it originates with a mind proud,
in deepest loyalty, to know that I can be esteemed. I have the
greatest desire to declare myself as
Your Majesty's
lowest, mot loyal and respectful servant
Antonio Vivaldi"

Incidentally, it has been determined that the printing must have originated already in the year 1708, since copies without the dedication were circulated. Vivaldi apparently acted quickly and wisely when the occasion to benefit from his works arose.

The collection "L'Estro Armonico," op. III (1711) made Vivaldi suddenly famous all over Europe. In the case of these concertos, it is equally wrong to take the year of publication entirely for granted. As the orders placed by Philipp Franz von Erwein indicate, concertos by Vivaldi must have been before the public as early as the first decade of the 18th century. Bach became acquainted with part of the concertos since the days of his activity in Weimar through the printed editions only. He arranged six of them for harpsichord or organ, incorporating the solo part. These are Nos. 3 and 8 to 12. One of them, the concerto for two violins in d minor, Op. III No. 11, would have made Vivaldi widely known, long before the famous-infamous Kreisler concerto, if it had not been considered a work by Wilhelm Friedemann Bach. The latter has actually passed off the manuscript which he had inherited from his father, as a composition of his own and thereby has stolen twice, once unwittingly from Vivaldi and once knowingly from his father. The Liszt pupil August Stradal edited it, believing it to be a work of W. F. Bach, in 1897 in an arrangement for piano for Breitkopf & Härtel. He added an informative preface to this unique document of his period, an arrangement of an arrangement.

Ill. 28: Title page of the piano arrangement by Stradal of the Bach organ arrangement of Vivaldi's Op. III Nr. 11

Ill. 29 a/b: (Following pages:) The first two pages of Stradal's piano cadenza to Vivaldi: Op. III Nr. 11

Cadenza ad libitum.

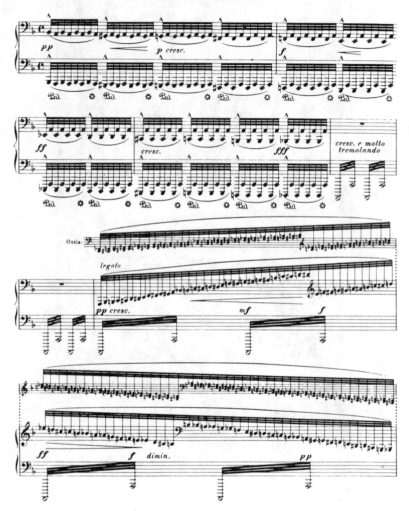

Ill. 29a

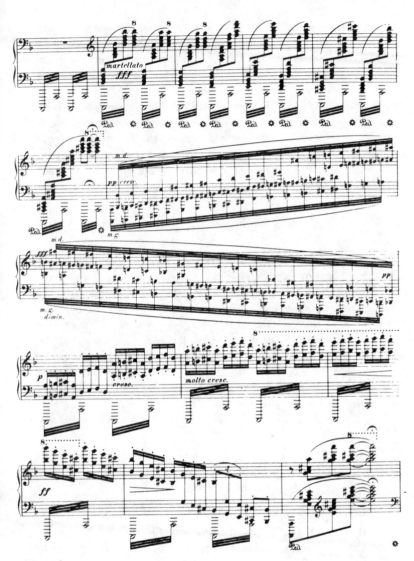

Ill. 29b

"The beginning of this organ concerto with its majestic pedal point in D and its great crescendo offered the opportunity and tempted me spontaneously to enlarge and extend the growing and rising forces of music. Furthermore, the slowly rising d minor chord seemed to me like a distant, nearly forgotten forerunner of the E flat major chord at the beginning of "Rheingold" by R. Wagner. Today's concert grands make it possible to play a crescendo from the softest ppp to the most powerful fff. Except for the introduction where several measures were added to the original, and the cadenza (which is ad libitum), I have followed the original strictly, trying to imitate the power of the organ with a full setting. . ."

The cadenza had been given a special preface by Stradal:

"I have adapted this cadenza to the stormy character of the work. The title picture gives the general tone of the concerto: "Storm, dark clouds racing across the horizon, lightning and thunder." The Nationalzeitung in Berlin wrote on the occasion of one of my concerts there: 'The performance of the organ concerto by W. F. Bach impressed me as a great natural occurrence. One saw mountains shaking and trees being uprooted by the storm.' I may add that I consider this organ concerto of the unhappy and unsteady W. F. Bach — perhaps a mirror of his own restless soul — the first forerunner, and entitled to be considered a real piece of art, of the marvelous storm fantasies by Beethoven, Wagner and Liszt."

"Storm, dark clouds racing across the horizon, lightning and thunder" are gracing the title page; the cadenza contains Lisztian piano cascades.

The fact that several numbers of Opus III can probably be traced back to the time when Vivaldi had close contact with the orchestra of San Marco may be assumed from the strange way of printing in four violin parts, 2 viola parts and one part for bass and figured bass, with the first violin having the notation "obbligato." This really was a setting for double chorus, as the architecture of the Venetian cathedral with the two choruses facing each other

The violin virtuoso

In a "Guida dei Forestieri in Venezia" (Guide for foreign visitors to Venice) in 1713, Antonio Vivaldi is named, together with his father, as an excellent violinist. When these visiting violinists arrived, the attraction was always Vivaldi's playing as well as his compositions. The report by Herr von Uffenbach quoted in the first chapter shows how Vivaldi's virtuosity impressed his listeners who had a high degree of professional knowledge and were not easily impressed. This virtuosity of his could not for quite some time be properly comprehended, since the compositions published during his lifetime did not show very much of it and, what there is, only in his later works. Probably, Roger was more interested in works with lesser technical demands on the players, in order not to discourage his customers. Therefore, an examination of the opera IV, VI and VII is revealing: there are more concertos like Op. IV No. 7 which are quite easy to play, rarely contain double stops and arpeggios and avoid to a large extent passages with pronounced technical difficulties for bowing. In Op. IV No. 6, there is a pretty passage in the last movement where it seemed necessary for Vivaldi to indicate the "zero" position through a fingering mark:

On the other hand, when Vivaldi was able in Op. VIII to present a magnificent title and had largely solidified his reputation as a composer of concertos, he could afford to place the concertos with the title "The Seasons" which are technically so interesting at the beginning, at the same time explaining and somewhat toning down the difficulties in the appended program.

shows. It made sense only for part of the (probably older) works, but was retained also for the (probably later) concertos.

In a note for the reader of Opus III, there is, incidentally, an announcement of Opus IV which appeared a little later. In this series, the transition to the typical Vivaldi instrumentation with solo violin and string orchestra (2 violins, viola, cello and figured bass), later mostly called "concerti a cinque," is carried through in the printing order as well.

The reputation which Vivaldi acquired through his activity at the Ospedale is indicated by a document addressed by the publisher Bortoli to the office of the censor, at the time when he wanted to print the fourth edition of the textbook by Gasparini "L'Armonico pratico al cimbalo:"

"The book contains the rules of music, also some observations about proper accompaniment on the spinetto or the organ in church. Authorities like D. Vivaldi who directs the music at the Pietà are full of praise. . ."

The growing fame abroad which was probably further advanced through tales and reports of visitors to Venice, is attested to by a number of visitors seeking instruction from the maestro. They were mainly finished musicians who sought new ideas for their violin playing and wanted to acquire a better idea of the solo concerto and its performance practice directly from him. Vivaldi was for them, as he said so well in the dedication of his Opus IV to "Sig. Vettor Delfino nobile Veneto," more a companion in their studies than a director ("più compagno nello studio, che direttore"). In 1712, Gottfried Heinrich Stöltzel, only 22 years old at the time, but already conductor in Breslau and successful opera composer, visited Venice. In April 1716, Pisendel, then 29 years old, arrived in Venice in the retinue of Frederic August III., the son of August the Strong, later on Elector of Saxony and King of Poland. As a pupil of Torelli, the excellent violinist was already expert in the Italian way of playing. There appears to have been a close relationship between him and Vivaldi; six concertos and three sonatas in the Dresden State Library carry the remark "fatto per il Sig[r] Pisendel." Hiller reports about an opera performance in 1717, where Pisendel played, at the suggestion of the Elector, the violin concerto PV268 by Vivaldi as entr'acte music:

> *"Once I was asked, at the suggestion of the Royal Elector's son and probably because at that time dances were not as customary in operas as today, to play in the orchestra during an opera performance between two acts a violin concerto (I do not recall, if at San Chrisostomo or San Angelo). He selected one in F major with horns by Vivaldi which begins in unison, as follows:*

> *"The last movement of this concerto begins like this:*

> *"In this last movement the concertino part starts with a cantabile solo. In the end, however, there is a long passage of thirtyseconds which are entirely positioned in the applicatura (where one has to change the position constantly). During this passage, the men in the orchestra, all Italians, tried to confuse Signor Pisendel by rushing the accompaniment. He did not let this bother him in the least, but kept those musicians who tried to set a trap for him in time by stamping with his feet, so that they were all ashamed in the end. The prince was greatly amused by all this. . ."*
> (J. A. Hiller: Wöchentliche Nachrichten. . . 1767/285)

The considerable inventory of Vivaldi works in Dresden — at one time it consisted of 87 concertos, 10 sinfonias, 17 sonatas, 3 motets and 10 cantatas — had its origin with Pisendel and the preference of his master for the music of

Vivaldi. A special treasure in the Dresden librar, certo by Vivaldi whose middle movement con bellishments in different versions. Schering assu Pisendel made notes of versions which Vivaldi him have played.

In 1716, Daniel Gottlieb Treu, better known Italianized name Fedele, was a pupil of Vivaldi. Th of Württemberg had sent him to Italy to study, so t could add some features of their performance pract Italian masters to his own orchestra.

Some other composers are presumed to have vi Vivaldi for instruction, since their works show traces of his influence. But these could as well be due in the case of Quantz, to the study of his compositions.

There is also the possibility that Vivaldi did not let those works be printed which showed his most violinistic daring, so that he could reserve them for his own repertoire. Such "business secrets" were quite customary from the time when the virtuosi became popular; Paganini also strengthened his dominant position in the world of violinists for a long time by the same procedure.

The works which were not printed during his lifetime contain an astonishing degree of virtuosic opportunities of all kinds and permit inferences as to Vivaldi's playing of the violin which had reached a considerable peak as early as the first decade of his activity at the Ospedale. He may have neglected it somewhat by the time he started producing his operas, and at the close of his life he no longer reached the former perfection on the violin. A passage by de Brosses written during his stay in Padua makes this clear:

> "We had to stay until the 31st, in order to hear Tartini who is generally considered the best violinist in Italy. It was worth the time spent. I have never heard such clean playing, where not one note is lost and there is total security. His playing is similar to Le Clerc and has barely any brilliance. Precision is his strength. In other respects, Anna-Maria of the Ospedaletto in Venice is his superior . . ."

(September 6, 1739)

The Opus III by Locatelli, the "XII Concerti cioe Violino solo, con XXIV Capricci ad Libitum," was published in 1733 and can be considered a new advance of Italian virtuosity in the direction of Paganini. The opinion was held for a long time that the work also influenced Vivaldi. But the virtuosity of Locatelli was made possible more on the basis of Vivaldi's playing and should not be considered as a late development of Vivaldi caused by Locatelli.

The decisive work is the violin concerto in D major (PV 165) by Vivaldi which carries the subtitle in the Dresden manuscript "Fatto per la Solemnità della S. Lingua di S. Antonio in Padova" and is dated 1712. Vivaldi may well have played it in Padua himself. The third movement contains a cadenza which is written out in full. The score has a notation in the beginning "Qui si ferma à piacim" (stop here ad libitum):

Adagio

tr

Orchestra enters

6 more measures

69

The bracket reaching from the second note of the 25th measure to the fourth measure from the end clearly indicates a transposition an octave higher, although it is placed below the notes. (This way of notating is also found in other works!) This proves that Vivaldi already used the 12th position in 1712. Incidentally, the f'''' sharp was beyond the fingerboard of those times, and the assumption is permitted that, at least for his personal use, he employed

Ill. 30 a

Ill. 30 b

*Ill. 30 a/b: Cadenza from the violin concerto in D major
(PV 165), third movement*

an extended fingerboard. It is highly possible that Vivaldi played this concerto as an insert at the opera performance in 1715 which Uffenbach heard in Venice. All the details of the description fit this cadenza which is most surprising for its compositorial disposition: it begins in 4/4 time, even though the third movement is written in 3/4 time, and changes after 19 measures temporarily to 3/4 time. The 4/4 meter is necessary, because motivic material from the first movement is taken up. The final cadenza was a "cyclical" one for Vivaldi in another previous work (PV 23), i.e., a cadenza which took its motivic material in part from other movements.

Ill. 31: Canaletto (1697–1768): Venice, Il Canale Grande verso Rialto

Another cadenza, this one from the violin concerto PV 14 in C major, shows an arpeggio entrance in the ninth position which is, however, violinistically very well prepared:

With the help of the given fingering (not originally by Vivaldi, but certainly conceived the same way), the rather tricky entry is well prepared.

In a Dresden concerto (PV 270) the composer demands in the first movement an interval of a twelfth. This is not performable for "normal" fingers on the violin, but it is introduced in such a way that the interval becomes possible by having the fourth finger stay set while the first gradually slides down. Here the realization is in a way included in the composition.

Vivaldi did not just seem to master the fingerboard without the slightest difficulty; he also was an expert of the bowing technique. Actually the bow underwent considerable changes during the first decade of the 18th century, anticipating in some details the later Tourte bow. In a picture of the young Tartini from about 1715, the older, slightly outward curving bow is shown, while another one of later years already indicates the bow with a slightly concave curve and a steeper tip which made the elastic back stroke possible for the first time. It seems that Vivaldi took part in this development, and only in this way many of the artistic feats involving the bow were possible, as in this example:

Of course, the most noticeable technical feats of his bowing are his staccati which are sometimes continued for up to 24 notes. Less obvious are the difficulties for the right hand in the many arpeggio passages where Vivaldi either leaves the execution open or indicates it by the measure introducing them. In the book "Performance Practices in Vivaldi" a number of cases occurring in his works are given which demand already quite a subtle bowing technique.

An example from the violin concerto in D major (PV 200) may offer proof of how close to Paganini the arpeggios of Vivaldi came.

His own virtuosity has influenced his entire musical thinking to a very considerable degree. Schering already has stated that his operatic arias have a concertante style and these instrumental tendencies in the opera are not

*Ill. 32: Matteo Gofriller (1670–1742), Venice 1700
(Walter Hamma, Meister italienischer Geigenbaukunst,
Stuttgart 1964)*

found with his contemporaries, for example with Albinoni
and Steffani.

Unfortunately, we do not know what kind of instrument Vivaldi played. There is scarce mention about his

relations with violin makers in the cashbooks, for example on March 12, 1708, also on April 6 and 23 of the same year, about the purchase of a viola, about viola d'amore strings, about a violin. A single notice of October 1, 1713 uses a name:

"a don Antonio Vivaldi per prezzo di un violino, deve servire per Susanna figlia di coro" ducati 18, "a Mattio Selles lauter per saldo di una viola consignata, deve servire per Maria figlia di coro" ducati 20.

This Mattio Selles may well have been a descendent of a Matteo Sellas who built excellent plucked instruments during the first half of the 17th century. But there is no doubt that Vivaldi personally dealt with the violin makers Matteo Gofriller (1670–1742), Domenico Montagnana (1683–1756), Francesco Gobetti (1690–1749), Petrus Guarnerius (1695–1762) and Sanctus Seraphin (1699–1744) who were active in Venice during his lifetime.

*Ill. 33: Domenico Montagnana (1683–1756), Venice 1729
(Walter Hamma, Meister italienischer Geigenbaukunst,
Stuttgart 1964)*

*Ill. 34: Petrus Guarnerius (1695—1762), ex-Wieniawski,
Venice 1723 (Walter Hamma, Meister italienischer Geigenbaukunst, Stuttgart 1964*

Ill. 35: Sanctus Seraphin (1699—1744), Venice 1732
(Walter Hamma, Meister italienischer Geigenbaukunst,
Stuttgart 1964)

*Ill. 36: Francesco Gobetti (1690–1749), Venice 1726.
(Walter Hamma, Meister italienischer Geigenbaukunst,
Stuttgart 1964)*

"Une furie de composition"

(An obsession with composing)

When Charles de Brosses stayed in Venice for a few weeks during the summer of 1739, his visit was, of course, also aimed at seeing Vivaldi. He reported about it on August 29 in a letter to his friend de Blancey:

> "Vivaldi has entered into a close friendship with me, in order to sell me his concertos at a rather high price. He was partially successful, but so was I, since what I wanted was to hear him and often spend wonderful musical hours with him: he is old now, but he has a surprising obsession with composing."

Such passages are often quoted during discussions of the "amoralità" of the composer, originating in the romantic attitude of a starving genius. Actually, Vivaldi was adept at using every possible means to make money from his compositions. It can be assumed that at a time when pirated editions were the custom, to have music printed by an honest publisher was not one of those means. We do not know what the fees were for a series of twelve concertos. Printing was absolutely necessary, in order to become known, and that was probably all the profit that resulted from the publications. A composer had to use other means, if he did not want to work hard barely to eke out a meager living. Since he was active at a center of foreign visitors, Vivaldi was offered the chance of contacts with the generally well-heeled travelers who visited him with the intent to acquire some concertos from him. In the diary of Uffenbach there are two characteristic entries:

> "Wednesday, 6 Martii 1715
> "After dinner Vivaldi, the famous composer and violinist, visited me, since he has often been told at his home that I had spoken about some concerti grossi which I wished to acquire and had ordered from him. I also served him, since he is one of the can-

tores, some bottles of wine, whereupon he produced his very difficult and inimitable fantasies on the violin. From nearby I was able to admire his ability all the more and saw very clearly that he plays extremely difficult and varied pieces, but had no pleasant and singing style of playing."

"Saturday, 9 Martii 1715
"In the afternoon Vivaldi came and brought me, because I had ordered them, ten concerti grossi which, as he told me, he had expressly composed for me. I purchased some of them, and to let me hear them better, he wanted to teach me how to play them and visit me occasionally for this purpose, starting this day."

Ill. 37: Francesco Guardi (1712–1793): Venice, La Piazza San Marco, detail

If Vivaldi said that he had "expressly composed" the concertos, this must be considered as just flattery toward a customer. But since his "business" was operating smoothly in any conceivable situation of his life, it appears quite believable that he wrote a few new concertos between March 6 and 9.

At the Vivaldi Congress in Venice in 1978, Michael Talbot disclosed a passage from a letter from Holdsworth to Charles Jennens, dated February 13, 1733 in Venice, which throws light on the business practices of a composer during the first half of the 18th century. It reads:

> *"I had this day some discourse with your friend Vivaldi who told me y^t [that] He had resolv'd not to publish any more Concerto's, because He says it prevents his selling his Compositions in Mss w^{ch} [which] He thinks will turn more to account; as certainly it wou'd if He finds a good market for he expects a Guinea for ev'ry piece. Perhaps you might deal with him if you were here to choose for you at that price. I had before been inform'd by others that this was Vivaldi's resolution. I suppose you know y^t He has publish'd 17 Concertos."*

(Gerald Coke Handel Collection)

Holdsworth inquired in Amsterdam about the correct number at the publishers and wrote a short time later to Jenners (Amsterdam, July 16, 1735):

> *Monsr la [sic] Cene who has publish'd Vivaldi's & Albinoni's works assur'd me y^t if you have 12 of Vivaldi's Op. and 9 of Albinoni, you have all. Let Vivaldi, he says, reckon as he pleases. He has publish'd no more than 12; and must count several of them double to make up the number 17. wch piece of vanity suits very well wth his character.*

(Vivaldi had counted the publication numbers: the Opera I, II, V, VI, X, XI, XII were printed in one volume each, the remaining Opera in two volumes each, so that the total — taking separate edition numbers — is exactly 17!)

There is some proof of the speed of his composing: it is the score to the opera "Tito Manlio," kept in Turin, on whose title page there is a note in his own handwriting "Musica del Vivaldi fatta in 5 giorni." And de Brosses explains on August 29, 1739:

"I heard myself how he offered to write a concerto with all parts in less time than it takes a copyist to transcribe it."

*Ill. 38: Johann Friedrich Armand von Uffenbach
(Engraving by Beer, 1768)*

Such a speedy production was absolutely necessary under the operatic conditions of the 17th and 18th century, if a composer wanted to do justice to all his duties. It happened quite often that an opera was booed off the stage — not because the quality was not good enough, but because of some intrigue and the well functioning claque made up of gondoliers —; in such cases, a replacement had to be produced at miraculous speed, and Vivaldi was quite often a friend in need. Sometimes, three composers had to combine their efforts in order to write an opera, each one act. On very urgent occasions, older works of one's own were borrowed from, even those of other composers. New texts were added and quite a few arias were transposed by an assistant. In a letter of November 6, 1737, Vivaldi mentioned another way of reducing the time needed to produce an opera:

> "Now, they are telling me, Coluzzi wants to dance in Venice this fall, something that is not possible on my part, since the composing of dances takes at least 16—18 days and the composition cannot be produced here in Venice, since the dancers are scattered all over. Therefore, I have engaged Catenella, a capable inventor who often works with Madame St. Georges. If Coluzzi really dances in the fall, her dances would have to be completed in five or six days, and that is impossible."

In order to understand this letter, one ought to know that steps and figures were first created in a ballet, and the ballet composer then invented the music, so to speak, to measure.

Ernst Ludwig Landshoff described the appearance of Vivaldi's handwriting nicely in the preface to his edition of the concerto PV 228:

> "Page after page reveals the temperamental sweep of a pen which grows more hasty as the writer is urged on under the pressure of increasing mental stimulus, the scurrying pen hardly seems able to keep pace with the inspiration driving it on. The clefs and the notation at the beginning of each line assume more and more

sweeping proportions; the florid sweep of the note-groupings and the lower curvatures of the treble clefs even spread themselves over the adjacent stave system. Many accidentals had been overlooked by this haste and were retrieved by revision and for lack of space had been inserted above instead of between the notes: Wherever possible, however, Vivaldi made use of a condensed form of writing."

Such abbreviations are constantly found in his scores, as in a sign meaning "Ut sopra" (as above). It was used to transfer the frequent unison passages to other systems. It was also too troublesome for him to write sharps; for this reason, he wrote D major as follows: ♯

The da capo sign also proved often helpful. The inner movements were generally accompanied only by figured bass, or he framed the solo section which only used firgured bass by two orchestra sections. In this manner, even concertos could be produced fairly speedily, when circumstances demanded it.

There was in general no chance to add time-consuming details as the realization of the figured bass. For various reasons, Vivaldi could do without the figures: for one, his harmony was relatively simple, especially in fast movements; also, he either sat at the harpsichord himself or had at his disposal Michielina del organo or Rosanna, Lucieta or Giulia who were all capable of executing Vivaldi's basses without figures. So there are in Vivaldi's manuscripts very many "unfigured figured basses!"

In a single case he carefully wrote down the figures and added the remark "per i coglioni" which is typical for his somewhat crude sense of humor (coglione has the double meaning of "fool" and "testicles"!)

However, one would be mistaken to assume that Vivaldi was an uncritical scribbler. On the contrary, his manuscripts show that he did — in spite of the speed of the creative procedure — subject his production to sharp criticism

*Ill. 39: Facsimile from the Concerto ripieno in A major
(PV 231), first movement*

through an extremely well developed artistic mind. The fact alone that a number of concertos has been handed down to us in two or even more versions, sometimes with different middle or final movements, proves that he knew very well how to judge their effectiveness. The most interesting are the crossed-out measures. In the cadenzas of the violin concerto KV 14 in C major, there is a change in harmony which occurs at first every four measures, then is shortened to every two measures and finally is strengthened, by crossing out single measures, to a sequence of single measures. In a similar manner, single measures or pairs of measures are often crossed out in arpeggio sequences, in order to make the harmonic sequence more compact. Often ritornellos were condensed by him, in order to retain the tension when they returned.

In the cello concerto PV 32 the word "Largo" in the middle movement has been crossed out and replaced by "And^e" (Andante), in the violin concerto PV 14 "And^{te}" was changed to "Ad^o" (Adagio). Some markings give rise to the assumption that they were entered later on, but probably they have to do with various performances of the same work. Occasionally, cuts have been opened up again, perhaps by adding "si scrive" or "si scrive tutto." A view at his working habits is permitted through a concerto for two violins (PV 190) in D major, where Vivaldi wrote down a tutti in unison, but at once found it too long, before even working on the bass and the other parts. A concerto for violin, oboe and organ (PV 36) "ò pure 2 violini et Hautbois" (or else for 2 violins and oboe) is surprising: the composer has written the harmonies in the upper organ system in one spot of the first movement, before even outlining the melody.

An especially attractive correction occurs in the final movement of a violin concerto in C major, Op. IX No. 1, PV 9. Because of forgetfulness during his rapid writing, Vivaldi did not remember the original key and modulated to b minor, a key which did not belong to the modulation conceived in this solo concerto movement. Noticing the error, he crossed out a section and used the harmonies leading him traditionally back to C major.

The formal construction of the solo concerto movement was:

Ritornello	principal key	(Orchestra tutti)
Solo I	principal key-dominant	(Solo + B.c.)
Repeat-Ritorn.	dominant	(Orchestra tutti)
Solo II	dominant-relative minor	(Solo + B.c.)
Repeat-Ritorn.	relative minor	(Orchestra tutti)
Solo III	relative minor-tonic	(Solo + B.c.)
D.C.Ritornello	tonic	(Orchestra tutti)

This was, of course, only one of the many possibilities. Vivaldi has altered the form with a great deal of imagination and hardly any concerto movement is like the others. Stravinsky and Dallapiccola are reported to have said that Vivaldi has written only one concerto, but that one 600 times. It seems that they did not give any serious attention to the composer. It is only natural that in such an enormous production much "run-of-the-mill music" (Paul Henry Lang) can be found; but Stravinsky should have been more careful, having borrowed during periods of total loss of inspiration from (forged) Baroque composers. Also, the weakest of Vivaldi's concertos is still superior to the arrangement of the six cello sonatas of the master by Dallapiccola. Malipiero, by comparison, was much wiser when he said during an interview:

> "But the musicians closest to my heart — if we call them that — are Gesualdo da Venosa and Domenico Scarlatti; also Vivaldi, but only in up to ten concertos." (NRMI 1967/124)

There is a possibility that Vivaldi worked out certain proportions mathematically. In several manuscripts numbers can be seen in the margin which are connected to the number of measures in the movements. Some, on the other hand, have nothing to do with the particular work, dealing probably with income and expenditures!

Studying the corrections permits a good insight into the structure of the personality of the master, for whom a light and flowing production was the essential precondition for his tremendous number of works. His brothers seem to have had the same light touch, if without any sublimation of the creative spirit, resulting in their getting involved repeatedly with the courts. Francesco, by profession a barber, was banned from Venice in 1721 because of some relatively harmless affair in the early morning, presumably after a night spent drinking. The same fate — banishment, and for three years — befell Iseppo, also a barber, when he hurt the messenger boy of a drug store in a street fight on November 9, 1728. In the testimony of witnesses the composer is mentioned in a strange manner. A witness recognized Iseppo as having been involved and said:

> "Iseppo, I do not know his surname; he is the brother of the famous red priest who plays the violin."

Antonio Vivaldi was still better known by the nickname inherited from his father during the years of his greatest fame than by his family name.

First opera successes

The impresario Vivaldi

In 1713, Vivaldi took a month off, doubtlessly in order to have his first opera "Ottone in villa" performed in Vicenza.*The fact that a clergyman who has up to that point written only instrumental music, turns to composing operas at the age of 35, is at first sight surprising. However, it was not at all strange for a priest in Italy during the 17th and 18th century to be active in the theatre. His model was his presumed teacher, the priest Giovanni Legrenzi who was the composer of 17 operas. That he gave up creating operas when he was appointed conductor at San Marco, is hardly due to the fact that it was not in keeping with his station, but rather for lack of time. Edward Wright who traveled through Italy in 1720/22 said that it was customary to see priests in the orchestra and refers especially to Vivaldi.

Vivaldi was perhaps introduced to the world of the theatre by his father who frequently helped out there and played regularly in the orchestra of San Grisostomo for some period of time. It is not improbable that Antonio himself occasionally played in these orchestra, and he may have acquired some practical experience there.

An impresario was, of course, anxious not just to recover the money invested in such an undertaking, but as much as possible beyond. Therefore, far reduced expenditures were the supreme ·law, grand choral ensembles were cut, and if a chorus was absolutely necessary, its size was reduced to the minimum. Equally, the rich

* The performance took place on March 17, the council decision only on April 30. Such approvals after the event, often found in the books of Pietà, can only be used with caution for chronological purposes.

colors of a full orchestra, as in "Orfeo" by Monteverdi, were only a memory from the old days. The orchestra was standardized with two violins, viola, cello (with doublebass) and a harpsichord for the realization of the figured bass; in an emergency, single strings had to suffice. If the stage action required it, at the most two flutes were added (alternating with oboes, played by the same musicians!), also two horns, two trumpets, timpani and bassoon. Such a group of instruments, caused by necessity, did have its advantages, since the work could be performed everywhere in this standard instrumentation. Thus, the impresario opera led to a certain economy of means which was not entirely detrimental.

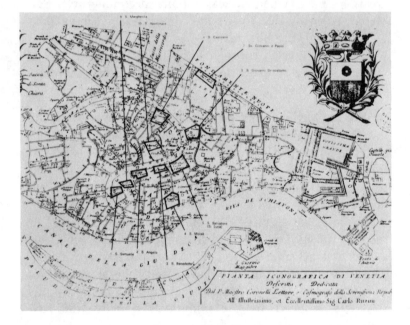

Ill. 40: Coronelli (18th century): Map of Venice. The ten best-known theatres of the city are marked on the map.

92

A sign of the Venetian enthusiasm for opera and theatre is the fact that during the 17th century there were no less than eight theatres which regularly scheduled opera performances. They are:

	founded
Nuovo Teatro Tron a San Cassiano	1637
Teatro Grimani dei SS. Giovanni e Paolo	1639
Teatro Zane a San Moisè	1640
Teatro di San Apollinare detto San Aponal	1651
Teatro Grimani a San Samuele	1655
Teatro Vendramin a San Salvatore	1661
Teatro Marcello-Capello a San Angelo	1676
Teatro Grimani a San Giovanni Grisostomo	1677

The Venetian operatic activities in Vivaldi's day had reached a peak which appears astonishing to us. In 1637, the noble family Tron inaugurated in their own palace, located in the borough around the church of San Cassiano, an opera theatre open to the general public. In the past, opera presentations were exclusively a matter for the nobility, mostly given at princely weddings or on other dynastic occasions. But now the entire population poured into the theatre. Somewhat later, there were as many as six opera houses, of which San Angelo was the most important for Vivaldi. (In Venice, the theatres were always named after the nearest church!)

While the princes were the patrons in the early days of opera, conditions changed considerably later on. The opera company had to be managed, and the noble patron handing out commissions was replaced by the impresario (impresa = business). He had to own a sufficient amount of money and his credit had to be good enough, so that he could sign contracts with everybody concerned. There were first the librettist, then the composer, the soloists, orchestra, chorus, ballet, the "ingegnere di scena" (stage technician), the "ingegnere di decorazioni" (stage designer), the "capo d'illuminazione" (lighting engineer), the remaining technical personnel down to the wardrobe mistresses, the make-up artists and the treasurers. Actually, there were no permanent theatres with regular ensembles; instead, performances took place during certain seasons (stagioni), i.e., the carnival or winter season from December 16 to March 30; the Ascension or spring season from Whitmonday to July 31 and the fall season from September 1 to November 30.

Ill. 41: Canaletto (1697—1768): Venice, Piazza San Marco

There were also several smaller stages performing operas occasionally. Such heavy activity with hard competition in a constant fight for the favor of the public made the highest demands on the composers, all the more so, since older works were rarely revived and if so, only after thorough revisions. During the period from 1680 to 1700, 150 operas were performed in Venice, or 7 to 8 works each season. From 1700 to 1743, which is approximately the creative period of Vivaldi, 432 operas were given which averages about ten each year. The figures for productions by some masters are astonishing. Carlo Francesco Pollaroli, for example, wrote 70 operas in 37 years and was at the same time organist, assistant conductor at San Marco and teacher at the Ospedale degli Incurabile!

This is the world of opera which Vivaldi entered and where he found fulfillment.* It can be considered as characteristic that his first opera was presented by him not in Venice, but in Vicenza. The smaller cities of Upper Italy served as a kind of tryouts for Venice. The performances must have been successful, since the work was repeated in Vicenza in 1715 and 1720, also in Treviso in 1729.

After having become firmly established on the stage with his "Ottone," there followed an uninterrupted series of operas at an average of two each year. It is hard to give a definite figure; as an example, "L'Incoronazione di Dario" which had its premiere in 1716 at the Teatro San Angelo in Venice, was the revision by Vivaldi of an opera by Freschi from the year 1684. By counting such revisions as works by Vivaldi, their number is naturally augmented. However, the authorship is not securely determined in the case of some works, and it may be considered as safe to

* For some time, it was assumed that Vivaldi presented an opera as early as 1707; but this date, found in a libretto, turned out to be a misprint for 1717.

In piazza de S. Marco semo avezzi
Fitar palchi ogni sera in sie teatri
D'Opera, e de Comedia a varij prezzi.

27

Ill. 42: G. Zampini (1789): "Le arti che vanno per via . . ."
man renting boxes

speak of about fifty operas. He asserted in a letter that he had composed 94 operas, but probably this figure included also revivals of older works. Counting all stagings in which he participated, one reaches the figure given by the master himself. He must have considered as "composto," i.e., composed or also put together, not just the compositions themselves but also arrangements and revisions. A listing of the stage works of Vivaldi is quite informative (see pages 101—106), since it shows the wide circle of his activities as an opera composer and the intense power of his works. The expression "operas by Vivaldi" is interpreted broadly here, including arrangements, single acts, etc.

In 1735/36, four Intermezzi by Goldoni were performed in Venice, for which the music may have been written by Vivaldi. They are:

Il Filosofo, 1735
Monsieur Petiton, 1736
L'Amante Cabala, 1736
La Bottega del Caffè, 1736

After the death of the composer his dramatic stage works were occasionally performed, among other cities in Vienna in 1742, in Hamburg in 1747, in Venice in 1750, in Braunschweig in 1767, in London in 1775. In most cases, they were pasticci with music by Vivaldi.

When Herr von Uffenbach attended an opera performance under Vivaldi's direction at the Teatro San Angelo in Venice in 1715, he wrote the surprising sentence in his diary:

". . . the impresario of this was the famous Vivaldi who also composed the opera. . ." (p. 67)

More detailed investigations by Giazotti yielded the fact that Vivaldi was actually the impresario of San Angelo as early as 1713, but had at first used somebody else as a figurehead.

De notte, ora ai teatri, ora al Redutto
Son quel che col feral serve de lume;
E pur che i paga mi so andar per tutto.

Ill. 43: G. Zampini (1789): "Le arti che vanno per via ..."
A man carrying a lantern accompanying visitors home
after the theatre

The fact is that Vivaldi turned to writing operas at the same time as getting into the business of running an opera theatre, i.e., the often rather shady sphere of impresarios. A contract still exists, signed by Vivaldi with the singer Lucrezia Baldini and dated October 13, 1726, and from the events of 1737 we learn how ably he took care of the business requirements.

The everyday events in the operatic life of Vivaldi, far removed from the attitude of the historians which was sometimes idealistically colored by the compositions, are described excellently in a satirical pamphlet "Il teatro alla moda" which appeared in Venice anonymously and without the year of publication. The detailed title reads:

"The theatre according to the current taste or a safe and easy method to compose Italian operas well and perform them in modern style. In it are necessary and useful instructions for poets, composers, singers of both sexes, impresarii, orchestra musicians, stage technicians and designers, comic roles, tailors, pages, extras, prompters, copyists, patrons and mothers of female singers as well as others attached to the theatre. Dedicated by the author of the book to his composers. Printed at Borghi di Belisania by Aldiviva Licante at the firm's nameplate of the bear in the boat. For sale at Coral Street near the entrance to the Palazzo d'Orlando. The book will be reprinted with addenda every year."

I L
TEATRO
ALLA MODA

O S I A

METODO ficuro, e facile per ben comporre, ed efequire
l'OPERE Italiane in Mufica all'ufo moderno.

Nel quale

Si danno Avvertimenti utili, e neceffarja Poeti, Compo-
fitori di Mufica, Mufici dell'uno, e dell'altro feffo,
Impreffarj, Suonatori, Ingegneri, e Pittori di Scene, Parti buffe, Sarti, Paggi, Comparfe, Suggeri-
tori, Copifti, Protettori, e Madri di Virtuofe, ed
altre Perfone appartenenti al Teatro.

D E D I C A T O

DALL' AUTORE DEL LIBRO
AL COMPOSITORE DI ESSO.

Stampato ne' BORGHI di BELISANIA per ALDIVI-
VA LICANTE; all'Infegna dell'Orfo in PEATA.
Si vende nella STRADA del CORALLO alla
PORTA del Palazzo d'ORLANDO.

E fi riftamperà ogn'anno con nuova aggiunta.

Ill. 44: Title page for "Il Teatro alla Moda"

No.	Title	Year and place of first performance	Librettist	Score preserved in: Libretto preserved in:	Remarks
1	Ottone in villa	1714, Vicenza	Lalli	Turin; Lib. Milan Vicenza	
2	Orlando finto pazzo	1714, Venice San Angelo	Braccioli, after Bojardo	Turin, Lib. Milan Venice	
3	Orlando furioso (I)	1714, Venice San Angelo	Braccioli, after Ariosto	Turin (Act 1 & 2), Lib: (an.) Milan	Revision of an opera by Ristori with music by Vivaldi
4	Nerone fatto Cesare	1715, Venice San Angelo	Noris	Lib: Bologna, Milan, Venice	Pasticcio with music by various composers, 12 arias by Vivaldi
5	La Costanza trionfante degli Amori e degli Odi	1716, Venice San Moisè	Marchi	Lib: Kremsler, Munich, Venice	later revisions
6	Arsilda Regina di Ponto	1716, Venice San Angelo	Lalli	Turin (2 versions), Lib: Bologna, Florence, Rome, Venice	
7	L'Incoronazione di Dario	1717, Venice San Angelo	Morselli	Turin, Lib: Bologna, London, Venice	
8	Tieteberga	1717, Venice San Moisè	Lucchini	Lib: Milan, Venice	
9	Il Vinto trionfante del Vincitore	1717, Venice San Angelo	Marchi	Lib: (an.) Florence, Milan	Presumably only cooperation by Vivaldi. Also performed as „Mitridate"
10	Artabano Rè de' Parti	1718, Venice San Moisè	Marchi	Lib: Milan, Venice	New version of No. 5
11	Soanderbegh	1718, Florence T.della Pergola	Salvi	Lib: Bologna	

No.	Title	Year and place of first performance	Librettist	Score preserved in: Libretto preserved in:	Remarks
12	Armida al Campo d'Egitto	1718, Venice San Moisè	Palazzi	Turin (Act 1 & 3), Lib: Florence, Venice	2 Arias in Act 1 by Leo
13	(II) Teuzzone	1719, Mantua T. Arciducale	Zeno	Turin, Berlin Lib: (an.) Mantua, Venice	Act 1 in 2 versions
14	Tigrane or The Victorious Constancy	1719, Hamburg		Lib: (an.) Berlin	Arias from No. 10
15	Tito Manlio (I)	1719, Mantua T. Arciducale	Noris		
16	La Candace o siano Li Veri Amici	1720, Mantua T. Arciducale	Silvani/ Lalli	Lib: Bologna, Washington	
17	La Verità in Cimento	1720, Venice San Angelo	Palazzi/ Lalli	Turin, Lib: Bologna, Florence, Venice	
18	Gli Inganni per Vendetta	1720, Vicenza T.delle Grazie	Lalli (?)	Lib: Bologna	Revision of No. 12
19	Tito Manlio (II)	1720, Rome T. Pace	Noris	Turin, Lib: Brussels, Dillingen	Act 1: Gaetano Bono, Act 2: Giovanni Giorgio, Act 3: Vivaldi (some nos. taken over from No. 15)
20	Filippo, Rè di Macedonia	1721, Venice San Angelo	Lalli	Lib: Florence, Milan, Venice	Act 1 & 2: Boneventi, Act 3: Vivaldi
21	Silvia	1721, Milan Nuovo T. Ducale	Bissaro	Lib: Bologna, Florence, Milan	Dramma pastorale
22	Ercole dul Termodonte	1723, Rome T. Capranica	Bissaro	Sinfonia and some arias: Paris Cons., Lib: Florence, Münster, Lund	

No.	Title	Year and place of first performance	Librettist	Score preserved in: Libretto preserved in:	Remarks
23	Il Giustino	1724, Rome T. Capranica	Berengani/ Pariati	Turin, Lib: Florence, Rome, Venice	
24	La Virtù trionfante dell' Amore e dell' Odio ovvero Tigrano	1724, Rome T. Capranica	Silvani	Turin (Act 2), Lib: Bologna	Act 1: Michele, Act 2: Vivaldi, Act 3: Romaldo
25	L'Inganno trionfante in Amore	1721, Venice San Angelo	Noris/Ruggieri	Lib: (an.) Florence, Milan, Venice	
26	Cunegonda	1726, Venice San Angelo	Piovene	Lib: (an.) Florence, Milan, Venice	possibly a pasticcio by Vivaldi
27	La Fede tradita e vendicata	1726, Venice San Angelo	Silvani	Lib: Florence, Bologna, Venice	
28	La Tirannia castigata	1726, Prague T. Sporck	Denzio (?)	Lib: (an.) Krimice, Prague	Arias by Vivaldi, partly from No. 5. Recitative by Guerra
29	Dorilla (in Tempe)	1726, Venice San Angelo	Lucchini	Turin, Lib: Florence, Prague, Rome, Venice	Melodramma eroici-pastorale
30	(II) Farnace	1727, Venice San Angelo	Lucchini	Turin (Act 1 & 2), Lib: Bologna, Florence, Venice	in 2 versions
31	Ipermesta	1727, Florence T. Della Pergola	Salvi	Lib: Bologna, Naples	
32	Siroe, Rè di Persia	1727, Reggio T. Ducale	Metastasio	Lib: Bologna, Modena, Washington	
33	Orlando (furioso II)	1727, Venice San Angelo	Braccioli	Turin (3 Acts), Lib: Milan, Modena, Venice	Act 1 & 2: in 2 versions
34	Ariodante	1727 Breslau	Salvi		Music by Pollarolo with arias by Bioni, Dreier, Orlandi and Vivaldi

103

No.	Title	Year and place of first performance	Librettist	Score preserved in: Libretto preserved in:	Remarks
35	Rosilena ed Oronta	1728, Venice San Angelo	Palazzi	Lib: Bologna, Florence, Rome, Venice	
36	Metope	1728, Breslau	Zeno		Pasticcio after 10 composers, among them Vivaldi
37	Griselda (I)	1728, Breslau			Pasticcio after 14 composers, among them Vivaldi
33	L'Atenaide o sia gli Affetti generosi	1729, Florence T. della Pergola	Zeno	Turin, Lib: Bologna, Milan	
39	Berenice	1729, Livorno T.S.Sebastiano	Lucchini		probably Pasticcio with music by Vivaldi
40	Agrippo	1730, Prague T. Sporck	Lalli	Lib: (an.) Prague	
41	L'Odio viuto della Costanza	1731, Venice San Angelo	Marchi/ Vitturi	Lib: Bologna, Florence, Venice	Revision of Nos. 5 & 10 by Galeazzi
42	Alvilda, Regina de' Goti	1731, Prague T. Sporck	Zeno	Lib: (an.) Prague	Music by Vivaldi except for recitatives and „le Arie Bernesche"
43	Semiramide	1732, Mantua T. Arciducale	Silvani	Lib: Bologna, Milano	
44	La Fida Ninfa	1732, Verona T. Filarmonica	Maffei	Turin, Lib: Bologna, Florence, Venice	
45	Doriclea	1732, Prague T. Sporck	Marchi	Lib: Prague	Revision of No. 5
46	Mo(n)tezuma	1733, Venice San Angelo	Giusti	Lib: Rome, Venice	

No.	Title	Year and place of first performance	Librettist	Score preserved in: Libretto preserved in:	Remarks
47	Sarce	1733, Ancona	Boldini		perhaps identical with No. 32
48	The Alchemist	1733, London	Jonson		Pasticcio after Corelli, Geminiani, Handel and Vivaldi
49	L'Olimpiade	1734, Venice San Angelo	Metastasio	Turin, Lib: Venice	some nos. from other works with changed text
50	(La)Griselda (II)	1735, Venice San Samuele	Zeno/ Goldoni	Turin, Lib: Rome, Venice	
51	Tamerlano	1735, Verona T. Filarmonico	Piovene	Turin (title: „Bajazet"), Lib: Rovigo, Milan	Vivaldi only cooperated
52	Adelaide	1735, Verona T. Filarmonico	Salvi	Lib: Milan, Verona	title disputed, perhaps identical with no. 38
53	Aristide	1735, Venice San Samuele	Calindo Gro-lo (Carlo Goldoni)	Lib: Milan, Venice	Dramma eroi-comico. Name of composer (anagram): Lotavio Van-dini
54	Ginevra princi-pessa di Scozia	1736, Florence T. della Pergola	Salvi	Lib: Bologna	
55	Partenope (also: Rosmira)	1737, Venice San Angelo	Stampiglia	Turin (title: Ros-mira fedele), Lib: Venice	Pasticcio, compiled after various composers by Vivaldi; in Act 1 arias by 5 compos-ers, among them Handel

No.	Title	Year and place of first performance	Librettist	Score preserved in: Libretto preserved in:	Remarks
56	Catone in Utica	1737, Verona T. Filarmonico	Metastasio	Turin (without Act 1), Lib: Bologna, Milano	
57	Didone	1737, London			with arias by Vivaldi
58	Demetrio	1737, Ferrara T. Bonacossi	Metastasio	Lib: Milan	opera by Hasse, edited by Vivaldi
59	Alessandro nell'Indie	1737, Ferrara T. Bonacossi	Metastasio		opera by Hasse, edited by Vivaldi
60	L'Oracolo in Messenia	1738, Venice San Angelo	Zeno	Lib: Rome, Venice	
61	Armida	1738	Palazzi	Lib: (an.) Rome	Revision of No. 12
62	Feraspe	1739, Venice San Angelo	Silvani	Lib: Milan, Venice	
63	Ernelinda	1750, Venice San Cassiano	after Silvani	Lib: (an.) Bologna, Venice	Pasticcio after Casparini, Vivaldi and Galuppi

Of course, the contemporaries knew exactly that the author was nobody but the composer Benedetto Marcello. A letter of Apostolo Zeno, written from Vienna in 1721, confirms this:

> *"The theatre according to the taste of Signor Benedetto Marcello is quite a delicious satire. . ."* (Letter to Fr. Marmi of April 2, 1721)

The year of publication can be determined by certain details in the book. In our day, the long forgotten author was rediscovered by Francesco Malipiero who found a copy by accident at an antiquarian's shop; in it, a reader had decoded in his handwriting the anagrammatic names. Even the date of publication, December 1720, is noted. The following persons play the leading roles in the satire:

Aldiviva = Antonio Vivaldi

Licante = Canteli, a female singer at the Teatro San Moisè

Borghi di Belisania = Borghi and Belisani, two singers at the Teatro San Angelo

Orso (bear) = Orsatto, impresario of the Teatro San Moisè

The booklet can hardly have done any harm to Vivaldi; it was read with enjoyment, one was pleased that for once such a successful man had been played a dirty trick, and then one returned to the day's business. The fact that the composer could be the center of such a satire after having written 13 operas during the first eight years, proves the position he had reached in the opera business. Incidentally, the pamphlet by Marcello was not directed particularly at Vivaldi; it lashed out with biting scorn at operatic conditions in general.

In speaking of the librettist, he considers it an advantage for him not to understand anything, or more than a little, about ancient dramatics; it suffices to express himself in

107

the preface at length about questions dealing with the text and quote Sophocles, Euripides, Aristoteles and Horace as witnesses.

The recipient of the dedication must be carefully selected; money is more important than knowledge, and it was apparently the custom to use an intermediary with whom one had to share the gratuity. Expressions like "libertà," "animo generoso" had to be used in the "Epistola dedicatorio," and at the end it was always advisable for the composer to kiss with deepest reverence the flea-bitten legs of the dog owned by the recipient of the dedication.

He considers it useful to get in touch with the impresario as soon as possible and ask him for his wishes. The number of scene changes does not depend on the dramatic demands, but on the impresario, and it is advisable in preparation of extended changes of scenery to lengthen the preceding scenes by dialogue, recitatives and ariettas accordingly. Arias should be of sufficient duration; it is best if the beginning is already forgotten by the time the middle section has been reached.

It is absolutely necessary to pay visits to insure the success of a first performance. Among those to be visited, the most important are the mother of the primadonna and her "protettore" (protector).

It is amusing to read Marcello's remarks about the composer. Too much knowledge of harmony is harmful; choruses and duets must be avoided, since they waste time. It is faster to use unison passages, octaves and pedal point a great deal. Italian overtures with elaborate themes and fugues are too much trouble; it is easier to write in the French style and with a dance as conclusion. But if an impresario is not satisfied with the score, he has to be told that it contains more notes than usual and that working on it took nearly fifty hours (Vivaldi's "fatta in 5 giorni" at ten hours each day!).

There are also rules for dealing with the personnel; special care is needed in dealing with castrati, and it is recommended that one follow them hat in hand. (Who does not recall the charming caricature of Schubert with the singer Vogl!) One should always keep in mind what illustrious personalities they may be called upon to play in the work.

Ill. 45: The only known authentic stage setting for a Vivaldi opera. Francesco Bibiena (or Giuseppe Chamant): The inside of the Teatro Filarmonico in Verona during a rehearsal to "La Fida Ninfa" by Vivaldi (Windsor Castle, Royal Library). Presented by Maria Teresa Muraro at the Vivaldi Congress in Venice, 1978. The following seven photos come from the same lecture.

Ill. 46: Contemporary stage design

Ill. 47 a/b (opposite page): Sketches for stage settings

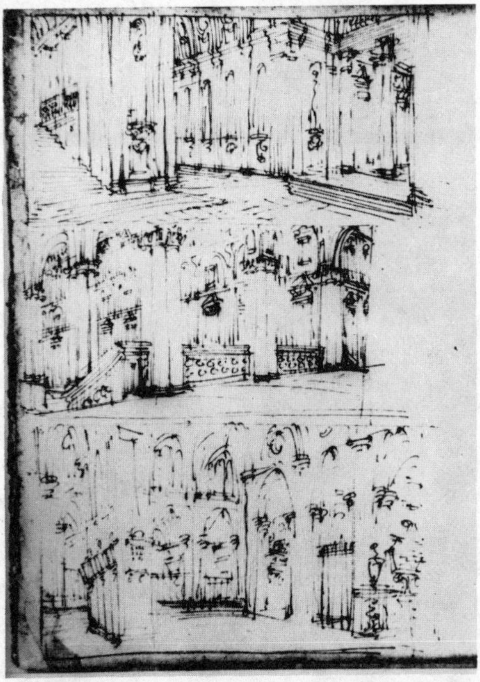
Ill. 47 a

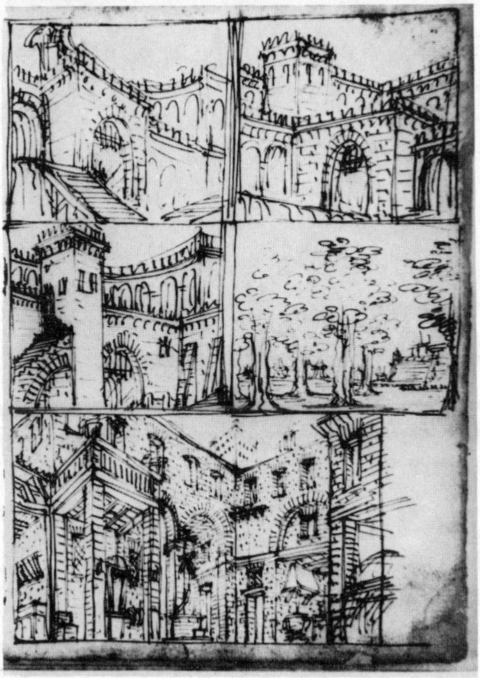
Ill. 47 b

Ill. 48: Stage setting. Sketch by Joseph Chamant, stage designer for the Grand Duke of Tuscany

Opposite page:

Ill. 49: Stage setting. Sketch by Joseph Chamant, stage designer for the Grand Duke of Tuscany

Ill. 50: Contemporary stage design

113

Ill. 51: Contemporary stage design

Ill. 52: Sketch for a "Deus ex machina"

Ill. 53: Contemporary stage design

115

Of course, the impresario fares very badly with Marcello. It is useful for him to have no specialized knowledge in any aspect of the theatre, but he ought to exert some influence on the form of the libretto and especially see to it that even tragic events have a happy ending. However, if two primadonnas are cast in a work — always a dangerous undertaking —, the librettist must be told that both get the same number of arias and recitatives and that even the number of syllables is identical for both of them. Incidentally, it is sufficient to hand the composer his commission eight days prior to the performance.

With the instructions for the impresario, Marcello touched on the field of operatic dramaturgy for which no written rules existed in those days, although there were, nonetheless, rules which were strictly observed. They were needed in order to make a speedy and numerically extensive production possible. Six or seven changes of scenery were obligatory, and every work had to have three leading roles. The same number of arias for these was absolutely necessary: an emotional one, a bravura aria, an "aria parlante," one of moderate characterization and a brilliant one. No more than three arias were permitted for secondary roles; at the most, two for smaller roles, but definitely no bravura arias. The primadonnas jealously watched over the compliance with these rules. Certain restrictions in compositions had as their underlying reasons just the avoidance of rivalries between the principal performers; for instance, arias of the same style directly following each other were not allowed, especially not two emotional ones.

The recitatives obviously were meant to save the voices of the singers and not to overburden the listeners. Actually people did not listen to them, but talked loudly in the boxes, ate, drank and played cards and board games. This

116

Ill. 54: C. Bodiani: Sala di giuco del Ridotto. Such gaming halls existed in the lobbies of the theatres.

activity was only interrupted when an aria began, but as soon as the applause started, they returned to their entertainment.

Under such conditions, masterpieces could hardly be created, but it is surprising how high the average nevertheless was and how important composers succeeded repeatedly in producing entire operas or at least some arias which even today are listened to with great interest.

It is questionable though whether Vivaldi was entirely happy in the world of opera. It may be a sign of the tension he lived under that he always returned, after excursions into this world, to the quiet work at his Ospedale.

117

Oratorio and church music

Until the Turin collections were discovered, the fact that Vivaldi had written church music was nearly unknown. It is easy to imagine the surprise felt by Alberto Gentili, when he found in 1926 in one of the boxes delivered to him four voluminous tomes containing sacred works, followed some years later by additional ones. Raimund Rüegge made a listing of the church music based on exact examination (Schweizerische Musikzeitung 1971/135—139), resulting in 47 works divided into the following groups:

> 11 works for chorus, soli and orchestra
> 6 works for chorus and orchestra
> 3 works for several solo voices and orchestra
> 15 works for soprano, strings and figured bass
> 11 works for alto, strings and figured bass
> 1 work for tenor, strings and figured bass

In addition, discoveries are made like the Warsaw Mass (University Library). Nevertheless, these figures will continue to remain approximately correct.

It seems that the turn toward opera, i.e., to larger vocal forms, went hand in hand with the creation of more extensive church music works. This development was favored by the illness of Gasparini for whom Vivaldi had to substitute (see the council decision previously quoted).

Ill. 55: Francesco Guardi (1712–1793): Venice, The
interior of San Marco

Ill. 56: Venice: Basilica San Marco, Iconostasi

Vivaldi wrote three oratorios which are of special interest to us, since they possibly point at parallels to the operas. They are:

1714   Moyses Deus Pharaonis/Exod.7/Sacra Poesis /Musicis Numeris concinnata/Ab. Admod. Rev. D. Antonio Vivaldi/In Brephodochio,/B.M.V./ Pietatis/Choraulicae Magistro/Cantabunt/Virgines ejusdem Brephodochii/Venetiis MDCCXIV/ Apud Bartolomaeum Occhium, sub signo S. Dominici,/Superiorum Permissu.
(performed in Venice in 1716)

1716   Juditha Triumphans/Devicta · Holophernis barbaric/Sacrum Militare Oratorium Hisce belli temporibus/A Psalentium Virginum Choro/in templo pietatis canendum/Jacobi Cassetti Eq./ Metrice votis expressum/Piissimis ipsius Orphanodicchi Praesi/dentibus ac Gubernatoribus/sub misse Dicatum/Musice expressum/ad Admod. Rev. D. Antonio Vivaldi/Venetiis, MDCCXVI/ Apud Bartholomaeum Occhium, sub signo S. Dominici.
(performed in Venice in 1716)

1722   L'Adorazione dei tre Re Magi al Bambino Gesù.
(performed in Milan in 1722)

Since the scores ot the first and third work did not survive, we are concentrating our analytical study on "Juditha." In the library of the conservatory Santa Cecilia in Rome, at least the libretto of the first oratorio has been preserved which contains handwritten first names of the female singers of the Ospedale. This list proves that the male parts were also sung by girls.

"Juditha Triumphans" is a "Sacrum Militare Oratorium," written to glorify the victory over the Turks which led to the Peace of Passarowitz (1716). The librettist Giacomo Cassetti applied the much-used material in a very concise and forceful manner: the beautiful and devout Judith is sent from the besieged city of Bethulia to the Assyrian commander Holofernes, in order to beg for mercy. As soon as he sees her, he invites her to a festive dinner in his tent which he celebrates alone with her. But when he falls asleep, she beheads him and saves the city. The high priest Ozias, speaker for the people of Bethulia, makes the connection of the theme with the city of Venice by comparing "Veneti maris Urbem" with Bethulia and calling Venice a "Nova Juditha."

In order to characterize the material, the beginning of the work has, instead of an overture, a "Chorus Militum furentium in acie" (a chorus of the soldiers spreading out during the battle), accompanied by trumpets and timpani (in addition to the string orchestra). Especially noticeable in "Juditha" is the rich orchestration. Vivaldi uses two flutes, two oboes, two "claren" (clarinets), two bassoons, two trumpets, timpani, a mandolin, four theorbos, viola d'amore, viole all'inglese, viola da gamba, strings, organ and two harpsichords. The orchestra is reminiscent in its colorfulness of the score to "Orfeo" by Monteverdi. Remarkable is the use of theorbos, since they were no longer in general use in Vivaldi's days. In 1685, there were four theorbo players in the orchestra of San Marco, and "Adriana, Stella and Maddalena dalla Tiorba" were mentioned in a 1707 document. Even a chorus from the distance ("Le Voci in lontano") is used. The work which has also been given designations like "azione sacra," had a scenic performance in Siena in 1939.

The arias are nearly always constructed like opera arias, i.e., they are similar in form to the solo concertos; an orchestral ritornello is repeated several times in different keys, and for the solo sections a solo voice, instead of a solo instrument, is used.

121

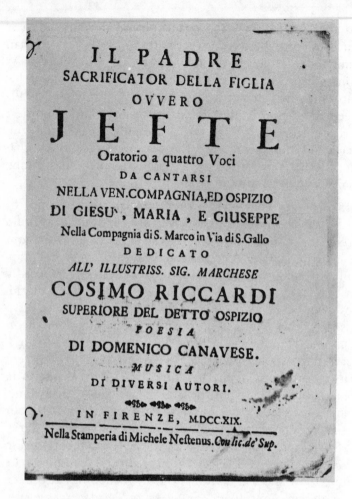

Ill. 57: Title page for the oratorio "Jefte"

An entertaining document was published by Ardengo Soffici in 1955 in the "Foglii di Diario" (Diary Leaves):

"Forte dei Marmi, September 8, 1944

"After dinner, I listened to the radio broadcast of "Juditha Triumphans" by Vivaldi. This was the first time that I heard music by this master. I discovered a genius of the highest order, with a beautiful work, stupendous. Greatest possible enjoyment.

"I am inexperienced in this field, I listen and understand just the masterpieces. The way I feel, this is one.

"If I were a musician, I would write music like this, just as I would, as an artist in a different field, work as a sculptor or painter like the Greeks or, among the later ones, like Donatello, Masaccio, Raffaello."

The list of oratorios can be extended. At the Vivaldi Convegno in Venice in 1978, Mario Rinaldi was able to furnish proof of a work "La Vittoria natale," performed in Vicenza in 1713, and Giancarlo Rostirolla gave information about the libretto of an oratorio "Il Padre sacrificator della Figlia ovvero Jefte" (Florence, 1720) which has been compiled with music of eleven authors: Palucci, Orlandini, Gasparini, Porta, Stuck, Mancini, Vivaldi, Scarlatti, Landi and Veracini, plus four other unnamed ("incerto") composers.

Basically, Vivaldi did not know any major difference between opera, church music, even instrumental music. This formal construction has, however, been enriched by beautiful choruses, in which the master fell back on previous styles. It barely seems possible that occasionally even older choral music was performed at San Marco and Vivaldi derived from it a wider range of expressiveness. As Manfred Bukofzer expressed it, he was like many of his contemporaries "bilingual," i.e., he spoke the musical language of his own times like hardly anyone else; but when the situation required it, he could express himself equally by means of the old vocal polyphonic style. This enriched his music through very special contrasts.

Among major church music, Vivaldi has mainly written settings of masses and psalms; they were broken down according to his rich musical gifts of interpretation and the separate sections were independently presented. The Gloria of the Mass which is divided into a twelve-part cantata may serve as an example of such an architectonic treatment of the text.

1. Gloria in excelsis Chorus, Trp, Ob, Str, Continuo	Allegro D major 4/4	
2. Et in terra pax Chorus, Str, Continuo	Andante b minor 3/4	
3. Laudamus te 2 Sopranos, Str, Continuo	Allegro G major 2/4	
4. Gratias agimus tibi Chorus, Str, Continuo	Adagio e minor 4/4	
5. Propter magnam gloriam tuam Chorus, Str, Continuo	Allegro e minor	
6. Domine Deus Soprano, Ob solo, Continuo	C major 12/8	
7. Domine fili unigenite Chorus, Str, Continuo	Allegro F major 3/4	
8. Domine Deus, agnus Dei Soprano, Alto, Tenor, Str, Continuo	Adagio d minor 4/4	
9. Qui tollis peccata mundi Chorus, Str, Continuo	Adagio a minor 4/4	
10. Qui sedes ad dexteram patris Alto, Str, Continuo	Allegro b minor 3/8	
11. Quoniam tu solus sanctus Chorus, Trp, Ob, Str, Continuo	Allegro D major 4/4	
12. Cum sancto spiritu Chorus, Trp, Ob, Str, Continuo	Allegro D major	

The trumpet in D is used to add brilliance to the numbers in the principal key. Meter and tempi are well distributed, just as the keys used are well balanced. As an example of Vivaldi's treatment of the chorus, some measures from the "Qui tollis" and from the "Propter magnam gloriam" are quoted (the instruments are strengthening the chorus). This passage could find a place in any of Bach's motets.

Ill. 58: Francesco Guardi (1712–1793): Venice, Rialto e il Palazzo dei Camerlenghi

Since copies of church music by Vivaldi were found in Bohemia and some similar works also in Dresden, the assumption has been that the vocal style of Bach has been directly influenced by Vivaldi. In particular, Bernhard Paumgartner who found in Florence a solo cantata "Piango, gemo, sospiro e peno," said in an article inspired by this (ÖMZ 1966/502):

> "This composition by Vivaldi is – as a parallel to Bach's knowledge of his instrumental works in the field of vocal music – undeniable proof of Bach's capacity for getting into the spirit of the vocal opus of the Italian master as a result of the discovery in Florence."

127

Ill. 59 a

Ill. 59b

This leads into a region where ingenious hypotheses are bound to have more weight than conclusive evidence. Jack Allan Westrup urges caution by saying:

> *"However, the comparison by Paumgartner was accepted by others and will no doubt find its way into the modest stream of history books of popular science, to be repeated devoutly by candidates at examinations . . . There is a great number of examples in Germany (take Graupner and Keiser). One can hardly exclude the chance that Bach has actually heard the cantata by Vivaldi. But there is no proof, and any suggestion of a recollection, even less of a real borrowing, is pure speculation."*
> (Music and Letters, Editorial, July 1969)

The church music of Vivaldi has probably exceeded in most cases the means available to him at the Ospedale. But we do know that he was more and more in demand, as his fame spread, to give a musical setting to major celebrations. Some of these occasions are clearly documented.

"Mercure de France" reports a celebration arranged by the French ambassador on the occasion of the birth of a princess. In the issue of October 1727, we read:

> *"A very beautiful instrumental concert lasting nearly two hours, of which the music, as that of the Te Deum, was written by the famous Vivaldi."*

In January 1732, he received a commission to write a "Laudate Dominum" for the transfer of relics into the Basilica of San Marco. Pier Zeno, the brother of Apostolo,

---

Ill. 59 a/b (opposite page): The Vivaldi manuscript of a "Credidi à 5 voci à Capella." The instrumental parts "à Capella" (!) had to be copied out by the copyist and the composer gave the following instructions: "The first violins must be taken from the alto an octave higher, the second from the soprano, the two violettas from the two tenors," with just the instrumental bass (cello and bass) realized because of the figured bass.

reports about the (open-air) performance in a letter to the Count Daniele Florio di Udine:

> *"On the banks the clergy of San Marco were waiting with burning torches, accompanied by the musicians playing a Laudate Dominum, a very solemn work of the Abate Vivaldi of the Pietà. . ."*

To prove what effect and appreciation the church music by Vivaldi has in our days, I should like to quote the remark of a girl student when I played a large-scale sacred work by Vivaldi at a musical quiz:

"This music is not actually by Bach, but it is good enough to have been written by Bach himself."

Ill. 60: Francesco Guardi (1712—1769): Venice, Processione notturna in Piazza San Marco

Concertos for various instruments

In a council decision of August 5, 1735, concertos for various instruments are mentioned:

"With their customary attention the directors, our representatives of the church and of the ensemble in the document read here in response to the order of this institute present as leader of the concerts the Rev. D. Antonio Vivaldi, a professional musician with the full competence of his office.

"Once the maestro has accepted the position, he must deliver the concertos for these our girls, also concertos for every kind of instrument, and he will have to be available, as often as necessary, to teach the girls and enable them to play them well. He is also obligated to instruct our girls in the best possible manner in the knowledge of those instruments they are playing whenever this appears necessary. According to this written document, the maestro is to receive a honorarium of 100 ducats.
With a majority

> *Abstentions 3*
> *No votes 2* } *accepted"*
> *Yes votes 8*

This document clearly defined that Vivaldi did not only have to compose the concertos, but that it also was his specific duty to prepare the girl soloists. This indicates that he must have been familiar with the playing technique of these instruments, possibly from his own experience. Incidentally, he was also temporarily nominated by order of September 20, 1720 as cello teacher:

"As suggested by the document just read to this institute by the kindness of the authorized directors of the church and of the ensemble, it appears to be absolutely necessary that there is, at least temporarily, a cello teacher available for this ensemble, in order to create total harmony in playing together. It is agreeable to make use of the Rev. D. Antonio Vandini (corrected to Vivaldi), *a priest about whom they have the best and most reliable references.*

"It is decided that the above-mentioned directors have permission to make use of the employment of this Rev. Vandini (read: Vivaldi) in this ensemble for some time. He will be paid with a fee set as per their attention, as long as it does not exceed 40 ducats each month. . ."

(The name Vandini which also appears in connection with an opera, has been corrected to Vivaldi in the document.)

Ill. 61: Report for the meeting on September 27, 1720, at which Vivaldi was selected as cello teacher (Venice, Archivio di Stato, Nottatorio dell'Ospitale della Pietà)

Therefore, the large number of cello concertos is not surprising, just as the astonishing selection of concertos for other instruments which Vivaldi offered to his girls.

The following is the total number of surviving concertos:

27	Vc	1	2 Fls
1	2 Vcs	16	Ob
3	Vn and Vc	3	2 Obs
2	2 Vns and Vc	1	Ob and Bsn
1	Vn and 2 Vcs	1	Ob and Vn
2	2 Vns and 2 Vcs	2	2 Obs and Vn
6	Va d'amore	1	Vn, Org and Ob
2	Va d'amore and other instrs.	3	Cl and other instrs.
10	Fl	36	Bsn
6	Fl and other instrs.	6	2 Hrns and other instrs.
2	Rec	4	Org and other instrs.
8	Rec and other instrs.	1	Mand
3	Flautino	1	2 Mands
		1	2 Trps

(Some of these figures are by necessity inaccurate; there is, to give an example, a bassoon concerto "ridotto per oboe" (arranged for oboe), a flute concerto with an arrangement for cello, etc. Some authors count these as two concertos each, others as single ones.)

The order of 1735 appears to be closely connected with the development of the wind concerto. Vivaldi may have initiated this around 1720 with flute concertos, perhaps followed by oboe and bassoon concertos. The decade from 1720 to 1730 would then have brought a growth of virtuoso wind playing by the girls at the Ospedale, finding its expression in the decision of 1735.

In terms of figures, the bassoon concertos are first on the list. We know through the report by de Brosses that this instrument was actually played by the girls of the Ospedale. If they played the solos in the Vivaldi concertos, they must have had an astonishing skill on their instruments which had only two keys. The range may not extend beyond the a', but runs, trills and especially the bubbling staccatos demanded the utmost from them. Passages like the one in the bassoon concerto in C major, PV 47, last movement are typical for the way Vivaldi wrote for the instrument:

In the bassoon concerto PV 49 he apparently felt that he went too far and added an easier version.

Next are the cello concertos, seven of which are preserved as rarities in the library of the castle Wiesentheid near Pommersfelden. They were perhaps written for the Count Franz Erwein von Schönborn who went to Rome at the age of 18 for his studies. Lessons on various instruments were considered a matter of course in the educational program, but we know that he hired a servant in Florence to carry his cello. Since his brother ordered for him on June 15, 1712 "about a dozen of the newest concertos by Vivaldi, Lotti and Pollaroli," one may take for granted that cello concertos were among them. The Wiesentheid concertos represent quite a homogeneous group; the demands which are of a lesser technical order let us assume that an amateur player ordered them. It is typical that in these works the string orchestra is barely used in the accompaniment of the solos; this was done in deference to the tenor-bass instrument whose sound may otherwise have been covered up.

The concertos written by the "cello instructor" Vivaldi are poles apart. Performing on this instrument received an impetus during these years, starting in Italy and finding expression in the solo suites by Bach. Vivaldi developed the technique according to that of his violin playing with staccato, spiccato and the use of the high positions. In the concert PV 180 he let the instrument go as high as f''' sharp; however, in the concerto PV 35 there is a passage which can only be played correctly by using the

134

thumb on the fingerboard. This means that Vivaldi may be the inventor of this use of the thumb on the fingerboard of the cello.

In connection with the cello concertos, 9 sonatas for cello and figured bass must be mentioned. Six of them were published in Paris and were announced in the "Mercure de Paris" in the issue of December 1740. Three more were found in Neapolitan archives and in the library of the Castle Wiesentheid. They are excellent pieces of exceptional elegance of rhythm and melody and make only moderate technical demands.

The oboe concertos were perhaps written for "Pelegrina dall'Aboè" who is mentioned in a document of the year 1707. A bassoon concerto, arranged for oboe, shows how Vivaldi realized the difference between the two instruments. The bassoon with its wider range makes special use of staccati and spread-out chords, while the oboe has melodic lines suitable for its character.

2nd movement (Andante, 3/4)

During the creative life of Vivaldi the transition from recorder to flute took place. There is naturally no definite date for this, and the two instruments were for a long time employed side by side, as in the case of Bach. Vivaldi probably wrote the first flute concertos and by so doing contributed to the gradual displacement of the recorder. It is typical that the Opus X "VI Concerti a Flauto traverso. . ." which appeared in print about 1728, contains works which are preserved in Turin in manuscript as recorder concertos. Vivaldi adapted some of them for the flute when preparing the printed editon. (As in Bach's works, flauto is the recorder, flauto traverso or flauto traversier is the flute.) In a "Salve Regina" for alto and double orchestra, the first orchestra contains two recorders, while the second has one flute which entwines the solo voice.

The "Concerto per flauto (i.e., recorder), oboe e fagotto" (PV 402) is a strange mixture of a trio sonata and a concerto. In the first movement the recorder plays the solo sections, but it is also taking part in the ritornello.

Vivaldi seems to have had very early a special predilection for the clarinet which in Venetian dialect was called "claren." It is used in the concertos PV 73, 74 und 84 and alternates in shorter inserts à due with the oboes. Anybody knowing the history of the clarinet would prefer to date these works later and if used earlier, take it to be a "salmoè." However, both instruments are used in the oratorio "Juditha" (1716), so that problems of terminology do not exist.

Ill. 62: Francesco Guardi (1712–1793): Venice, La Chiesa della Salute

In the matter of more rarely used solo instruments, it would help to know the name of the person commissioning or proposing the work. By chance, it is known in the case of the two mandolin concertos PV 133 and 134 that the Marchese Guido Bentivoglio in Ferrara played this instrument and that both works are perhaps dedicated to him. Vivaldi wrote him on December 26, 1736:

"Your Excellency may want to let me know, if you are still enjoying yourself on the mandolin."

Ill. 63: Antonio Vivaldi. Engraving by F.M.La Cave 1724

The composer used the instrument already in the oratorio "Juditha" in an aria as obbligato solo instrument. All these compositions have excellent instrumentation; the figured bass is often silent in the solo passages, the bass is, for instance, entrusted to a "Vio^{lo} Solo" (cello alone) or to the violins or violas. In the subtitle, directions for this are given:

"One may play this also with all strings pizzicato."

Thus, the orchestra acquires for extended passages a sound "à la mandolinata!"

It is constantly surprising how frequently the name Vivaldi appears on concert programs and record labels. The explanation is quite simple: he has written so many concertos for instruments which were neglected by his contemporaries, but are nowadays available in a wide assortment of editions, so that ambitious soloists are now gratefully making use of them.

Secular vocal music

Various contemporary reports show that in spite of limitations imposed on Vivaldi by the condition of his health, he took part in private social gatherings, accepted commissions to compose for such occasions and formed the center of smaller secular celebrations through his works. Serenades were especially popular on these occasions.

In 1722, a serenade was given at the Marquis Martinengo, another was written "Pour Monsieur le Mar. de Toureil," yet another was performed in 1726 in Mantua on the birthday "del Langravio di Assia-Darmstad."

We hear from Rome in 1723:

"The Venetian Signor Vivaldi has written the arias to texts of His Eminence Mons. Barbieri who gave him 100 scudi. They are sung at the house of Prince Colonna where the Imperial ambassador also visited."

Mons. Barbieri was secretary to Pope Benedict XIII., and it is probable that he arranged for them to be played also before the Pope.

In the end, Vivaldi was denounced in February 1740 at the inquisition, because he played the accompaniment for Anna Giraud on the harpsichord at a party at the Spanish ambassador until 3 o'clock in the morning. . .

It is difficult to give exact figures for the secular vocal music, since the categories overlap considerably. Some cantatas are, to give an example, surely arias arranged from lost operas and should therefore be considered among the separate arias. Girard counts 49 cantatas, 5 serenades and 61 arias; Demoulin counts 9 serenades, among them "Il Mopso" (Egloga pescatoria), Ryom 8 serenades and 38 cantatas.

The most important work in this group is doubtlessly the two-part cantata "La Sena festeggiante" (The celebrating Seine) on a text by Domenico Lalli. It begins with a Sinfonia à la francese, and an overture introduces the second part. Two allegorical figures, "L'Età dell'Oro" (The Golden Age, Soprano) and "La Virtù" (Virtue, Alto) are looking for the lost human happiness, reach the banks of the Seine and, of course, find it here. The Seine is represented by a river god, a very low bass. The work contains in its first part twenty numbers, in the second part fifteen. The composer asks in the orchestra occasionally for "2 Hautbois ò più se piace" (2 oboes or more ad libitum) and "Flauti ò più" (2 flutes or more), indicating possibly an open-air performance.

The years of traveling

Peak of his operatic activity

Vivaldi remained in Venice, except for his one-mouth excursion to Vicenza, until close to his fortieth year. At first, he was active at the Ospedale, later on also in his capacity as impresario of the Teatro San Angelo. During the following twenty years, his reputation as an opera composer made him undertake continuously journeys whose destination, duration and timing are only vaguely known to us. In addition, he was absent for long periods to fulfill official obligations. The list of stage works provides some clues, since it can be assumed that he was attending them mostly in person. Such a list also gives clues as to his presence in Venice, for instance during the years 1725—1728.

He gave some hints in his letters to Marchese Bentivoglio which are of considerable autobiographical interest. He wrote on November 16, 1737:

"In Mantua, I was in service with the most generous Prince of Darmstadt for three years."

Many conjectures were made about the timing of this stay. After a thorough investigation of all the documents Giazotti came to the conclusion that the service must have occured during the years 1718—1720, with an opera performance in Venice still taking place in 1718.

On the title page of the libretto to the opera "Verità in Cimento" Vivaldi called himself "Maestro di Cappella, di Camera di S.A. il Sig. Principe Filippo Langravio d'Hassia Darmestat," and he used this title occasionally in later years. For a long time, it was believed that he had connections with Darmstadt, but it concerned a brother of the reigning prince in Darmstadt, Margrave Philipp von Hessen-Darmstadt who captured Mantua as general of the Imperial forces and became commanding general of the occupying forces in Naples later on. From 1714 to 1735, he again resided in Mantua. The period of service was interrupted for Vivaldi by opera performances away from Mantua; he stayed in Venice for the performance of "La Verità in Cimento" and in Vicenza for the opera "Gli Inganni per Vendetta."

A cantata with the dedication "In lode di Monsignor Di Bagno, Vescovo di Mantua ' (In praise of. . .) refers to his stay in Mantua. The recipient of the dedication was appointed Archbishop in 1719.

Mantua was fateful for the composer, since he met the singer Anna Giraud there (in Italian, the name was spelled Girò). She was presumably born in Mantua as the daughter of a French wigmaker and was referred to on theatre programs often as "mantovana." She also was possibly a pupil at the Ospedale della Pietà in Venice where she was known by the name "L'Annina della Pietà," while later on she was only called "L'Annina del preto rosso." In the meeting with Vivaldi described by Goldoni, Vivaldi expressly called her his pupil which is not really surprising, since a close acquaintance with the technique of singing was part of the trade of an opera composer up to the days of Verdi. She made her debut in Venice in 1724 in the opera "Laodicea" by Albinoni. According to contemporary accounts, she was a singer of musicality and intelligence with a voice of moderate size, a deficiency compensated for by her acting ability. She appeared in works by Vivaldi from 1725 on.

Ill. 64: Pier Leone Ghezzi: "Il Preto rosso Compositore di musica che fece l'opera a Capranica del 1723"

Vivaldi wrote in a letter of November 16, 1737 to Bentivoglio:

> *"I was in Rome for three carnival seasons, in order to perform operas. . . I played in the theatre and it is known that His Holiness had the desire to hear me and that I received many marks of favor."*

These sojourns in Rome can be ascertained from the list of operas. He performed his opera "Ercole sul Termodonte" at the Teatro Capranica in 1723, "Il Giustino" and "La Virtù trionfante" in 1724; in the case of the latter only Act 2 is by Vivaldi. It has not been determined, before which Pope he played; primarily, Innocence XIII. must be considered, but Benedict XIII. who was elected Pope in May 1724 is another possibility.

The vivid caricature by P. L. Ghezzi was created during his first period of activity in Rome; it is kept in the Vatican Library in Rome (Cod. Vat. Ottoboni 3114f. 26). The caption reads:

> "The redhaired priest, composer, who does the opera of 1723 at the Capranica."

A trip to Vienna is documented which he mentioned himself in a letter of November 16, 1737 ("I have been called to Vienna."). Vivaldi did not mention the time, but a request by his father has been preserved possibly referring to this trip to Vienna:

> "Today's date, September 30, 1729
> "Since the violinist Giovanni Baptista Vivaldi asks for the generous permission to get leave of absence from the service in the Ducal orchestra, because of a trip to Germany to accompany one of his sons, with Francesco Negri substituting for him, his superiors have decided to grant him the requested permission for one year. In case he does not return at the end of the year, his name will be removed from the paybook. However, the precondition is that he is replaced during this period by above-mentioned Negri whose ability is known to the conductor."
> (State Archive Venice — Procuratori de Supra, Chiesa di San Marco — Reg. 153, Decreti e Terminazioni, c. 117t).

Ill. 65

Ill. 66

Camera nella Reggia Capranica

Ill. 67

Ill. 65, 66, 67: These three illustrations originate in a series by Filippo Juvarra: Cinque Pensieri per scenografie al Teatro Capranica di Roma, drawn between 1707 and 1715.

Since "Germania" included Austria in its meaning in those days, Antonio may have been in Vienna with his father.

In any case, there appear to have existed very close relations with the Austrian Emperor Charles VI., to whom the opus IX has been dedicated, as the correspondence of Abate Conti with Madame Caylus shows (letter of September 19, 1728). He refers twice to Vivaldi:

"The Emperor is not very well satisfied with his Trieste. . . . The Emperor conversed with Vivaldi extensively about music; it is said that he talked with him in 14 days more than with his ministers in two years. . . His interest in music is very considerable. . ."

"The Emperor gave Vivaldi a great deal of money as well as a chain and a gold medallion, and tell him also that he has made him a knight. . ."

It is possible that Vivaldi also went to Prague where an Italian opera company led by Antonio Denzio had performed about 60 operas by Venetian composers for the last ten years. The moving spirit behind this cultivation of opera in Prague was Count Anton Sporck who adapted his palace in Prague for this company which was engaged in 1724. They also used rooms in his summer residence Kukas and in Karlsbad. The performances of Vivaldi's works by the Denzio company began in 1726 with the otherwise unknown opera "La Tirannia castigata," whose anonymous libretto is preserved in Prague, possibly the work of Denzio himself. From the spring of 1730 on until the spring of 1732, no less that five operas by Vivaldi were performed, partly revisions of older works, partly operas whose titles are only known through the performances in Prague, among them "Alvilda, regina de' Goti" (1731) und "Doriclea" (1732). The latter is probably based on "La Costanza trionfante" of the year 1716 which Vivaldi had revised twice before in Italy. The last opera by Vivaldi was performed in Prague in the spring of 1732; it was "Dorilla in Tempe," written in 1726.

Ill. 68: Title page of the libretto to the opera "Doriclea" by Vivaldi, Prague 1732

Another contract of service which is open to question appears first in the libretto of an opera "Adelaide" which was performed during the carnival of 1735 in Verona. It says there:

> *"The music is by Don Antonio Vivaldi, conductor of His Highness the Duke of Lorraine and His Highness the Prince Philipp of Hessen-Darmstadt."*

The Duke of Lorraine resided in Florence. Vivaldi's visits to this city can be deduced from the opera listing: in 1727 for the performance of the opera "Ipermestra," in the following year for "Atenaide" and in 1736 for "Ginevra, principessa di Scozia." It seems that Vivaldi functioned as "house composer," i.e. he delivered works for the ducal orchestra from wherever he happened to be staying and was personally present only on some occasions.

A similar contract of service existed in relation to the Count Venceslav Morzin, hereditary Prince of Hohenelbe, to whom the opus VIII containing The Seasons is dedicated. In the preface, Vivaldi refers to his long years of activity in the service of this count:

> *"Most Serene Sir,*
> *"Thinking about the many years during which I enjoyed the much appreciated honor of serving Your Highness as music master in Italy, I blush thinking that I have not yet given a sign of my deep respect. Therefore, I decided to have the present volume printed and to put it at the feet of Your Highness. I hope that Your Highness will not be surprised to find among these few and insignificant concertos the "Four Seasons" concertos which have been accepted long ago by the noble generosity of Your Highness. However, I think I have acted correctly in having them printed, even though they are the same. They have been enlarged, apart from the sonnets, by a very detailed explanation of all treated happenings, and I am sure that they will appear all new to Your Highness. I do not want to hold forth in great detail asking Your Highness to look with a lenient eye at my weaknesses, because I believe I would insult the innate kindness with which Your Highness has accepted them for such a long time. The very great understanding which Your Highness has for music as well as the quality of your excellent orchestra*

150

*will always assure me that my poor efforts will, as soon as they
reach your much esteemed hands, enjoy such distinction as
they hardly deserve. There is nothing left for me but to ask
Your Highness for your continued generous protection and to
beg that the honor is never taken away from me to be always*

*Your Highness's
obedient and respectful
very devoted servant
Antonio Vivaldi"*

The longest trip of his life was undertaken by Vivaldi
when the centennial of the building of the Stadshouwburg
was celebrated in Amsterdam on January 7, 1738. The
invitation which must have been issued by the successors
of his old publisher Roger, was surely a matter of great
satisfaction for the master, since his worldwide reputation had started in Amsterdam. The program has been
preserved together with the orchestra list. Vivaldi had at
his disposal the following musicians:

7	Violins I	2	Bassoons
5	Violins II	2	Trumpets
2	Violas		Timpani
2	Cellos		Harpsichord
2	Contrabasses		

In addition to works by other composers, he played
one work of his own, the concerto grosso PV444.

Ill. 69: Orchestra list of January 6, 1738 in Amsterdam on the occasion of the centennial celebration of the opera (De Schouwburg von Amsterdam en zyn oude en niewe toonelen beeschrieven met deszelfs eeuwgetyde, geviert den 7 van Louwmaand 1738, Amsterdam, University Library)

Ill. 70: Facsimile of Sonetto Dimostrativo for the Concerto Op. VIII No. 2 (The Summer), PV 336.

Ill. 71: Scuola Veneta del 700: Laguna gelata nel 1788

The question arises how the management of the Ospedale felt about the approximately 20 years of Vivaldi's
traveling. The curious fact must first be mentioned in this
connection that Vivaldi had adversaries among the directors of the institution right from the beginning. Already
at the time when Gasparini asked for the violin teaching
position in 1703, there were two no votes and one ab-
stention versus eight yes votes. When Vivaldi was to be-

come maestro di viola all'inglese, there were nine assenting votes, with one opposing. Such bodies are by experience mostly subject to intrigue, covered up anonymously through seemingly democratic elections. Apparently there was somebody among the directors who wanted revenge for "his" candidate not having been nominated at that early date. When the election took place in 1706, Gasparini as "maestro di coro" received all ten votes, while there were three no votes in the case of Vivaldi. The voting on February 24, 1708 turned out even worse, when Gasparini again received all 13 votes and the result for Vivaldi was 7 vs. 6, so that a second ballot became necessary due to the closeness of the vote, having an even worse result of 6 vs. 7 against the maestro. The management decided, in other words, against the smooth operation of the institution! The fact that Vivaldi actually continued to teach in spite of this result, was obviously due only to their needing him badly. Perhaps the girl students who surely were enthusiastic about their maestro made the difference.

Finally, there was another vote taken on September 27, 1711, and the minutes read as follows:

"On the above-mentioned date (September 27, 1711)
"Realizing the necessity of giving the girls of the ensemble continuously better instruction in playing their instruments, in order to raise the reputation of this institution and because the position of a violin teacher is vacant.
"It has been decided that Don Antonio Vivaldi is accepted as violin teacher with a salary of 60 ducats a year. The institution is certain that he is capable of doing everything possible to serve this institution well and of being of greater usefulness to its girls.

Abstentions	0
No votes	0	accepted"
Yes votes	11

Vivaldi received all eleven votes. Did this vote express the effect of his concerts in Amsterdam?

On July 2, 1723, there was finally that meaningful document, found in the books containing the minutes, which was to settle the totally disturbed relations with the institution. Chorus and orchestra had become world-famous, and it was well-known that it was not alone due to the compositions of the maestro, but also to his teaching, the rehearsing (three times weekly) and the conducting of the performances that this generally esteemed quality resulted. Everybody knew also that he could no longer be tied down and took precautions so that his name continued to be associated somehow with the institution, even when he was absent. The document reads:

". . . *The exact document just read shows that, in order to keep the above-mentioned ensemble in as high repute as it has reached up to the present, the supplying of instrumental concertos is necessary, and it has been established that the custom is to be retained to have — as so diligently shown — two concertos written each month by the well-known activity of the Rev. Don Antonio Vivaldi, just as two were written for the current feasts of this our church. Therefore, it has been decided that the above-mentioned directors are given the authority to make arrangements with the above-mentioned Vivaldi for the time he is staying in this city and also when he is traveling, to see to it that the two concertos he obligates himself to supply each month are delivered by messenger, as long as he can mail them without charging postage. . ., on condition, however, that said Vivaldi teaches the girls at least three or four times in person for each concert in such a way that they perform them well, whenever he is in Venice. . .*

With the two-third majority

Abstentions	1	
No votes	0	presa"
Yes votes	9	

During the years 1724 to 1734 the name of Vivaldi is missing from the minutes of the meetings as well as from the cashbooks (although four volumes of them are lost).

Ill. 72: Report about the meeting of July 2, 1723, in which the contract conditions were newly settled (Venice, Archivio di Stato, Nottatorio dell'Ospitale della Pietà).

On August 5, 1735 the name reappears, but the tone has changed (see the text of the document at the beginning of the chapter about Concertos of various instruments).

The opposing votes grew again during the next years, as for example on March 28, 1738:

> *"Rev. D. Antonio Vivaldi Maestro de Concerti*
>   7 yes votes, 4 no votes"

Because of the large number of no votes, another ballot had to be taken (the vote was taken because of various pending matters); but the opposing votes remained stubborn, and it ended again with 7 vs. 4.

As opposed to this, the esteem in the world of violinists remained high: there is hardly one of them who did not benefit from playing Vivaldi concertos. A few examples may suffice; Burney (III/95) reports about Franz Benda (1709–1786) wo had started early playing the violin:

> *"It must, however, have happened early in his youth, since he remembers having played the viola during the concerts given by the choir boys in Dresden for their own pleasure, and that he had to work hard on the concertos by Vivaldi."*

Benda himself adds to this in his autobiography:

> *"At the same time, I practised on the violin and played the Vivaldi concertos of those days from memory."*
> (Lorenz: Franz Benda, p. 141)

Burney reports further (IV/660) that the violinist John Clegg, at the age of nine, played a violin concerto in London and that Guignon performed the "Spring" concerto in Paris in 1728.

In 1725 an anonymous contributor writes in the "Giornale dei Litterati:"

> *"Your style of playing the violin is rather advanced, as the music of the violinist Vivaldi shows."*

Gerber says that concertos by Vivaldi had a decisive influence for more than 30 years in this art form (Schering

GIK 96). The responsible authorities at the Ospedale, however, did not seem to have been aware of all this.

During his years of traveling, Vivaldi was also considered as the highest authority in questions dealing with operas. When Denzio assembled his company and needed to complement it with good people from Venice, he always turned to Vivaldi. In his book about Count Sporck, H. Benedikt writes about the year 1725:

> *"Denzio reports that he hired instead of Giusti the soprano Chiara Orlandi and instead of Vida the tenor Novello, both through Antonio Vivaldi in Venice. He is still negotiating through Vivaldi with the contralto Peruzzi from Venice."*

Quantz reports from Rome in 1724:

> *"The latest I heard was the so-called Lombardian style which was entirely unknown to me so far. It has been introduced a short time ago by Vivaldi through one of his operas in Rome, and it has influenced the people there to such a degree that they scarcely wish to listen to anything not resembling this style. However, it caused me quite a lot of trouble at first to find it agreeable and to get used to it, until I finally found it advisable to go along with this fashion."* (Autobiography, p. 225)

This is historically not entirely true, but it does represent the impression which the stay in Rome made on Quantz.

Further, the Abbé Conti tells in a letter from Venice to Madame Caylus, dated February 23, 1727:

> *"Vivaldi has written three operas in less than three months, two for Venice and the third for Florence. The latter has reestablished the theatre of that city and brought him a lot of money."*

In 1735 the meeting with Carlo Goldoni (1707–1793) took place which is of such great importance for the biography of the composer, because Goldoni devotes to it several pages in his "Mémoires, pour servir à l'histoire de sa vie, et à celle de son Théâtre." Goldoni who was 28 years old at the time, was for a long period undecided between the vocation of lawyer and the avocation of a writer of comedies. The "Mémoires" were written during the 1780's in Paris in French, were dedicated to the King of France and appeared at the publishing house of the widow Duchesne in 1787.

Ill. 73: Canaletto (1697–1768): Venice, Il Bacino di San Marco

(from part I, chapter XXXVI)
"The nobleman Grimani, owner of the Teatro di San Samuele, had an opera played at his theatre at his own expense, and having promised me to engage me for this undertaking, he kept his word.

160

"It was not a new drama which was to be given this year; "Grisel-da" had been selected, an opera by Apostolo Zeno and Pariati who collaborated before Zeno went to Vienna in the service of the Emperor. The composer who was to set it to music was Don Vivaldi who was called "preto rosso" because of his hair color. He was better known by his nickname than by his family name.

"This priest, an excellent violinist and average composer, had educated Miss Giraud, a young singer, and also had given her vocal instruction. She was born in Venice [here Goldoni was in error!], but the daughter of a French wigmaker. She was not beautiful, but graceful, had a lovely figure, pretty eyes, attractive hair, an enchanting mouth, not much voice, but a good stage presence. She was to play the role of Griselda.

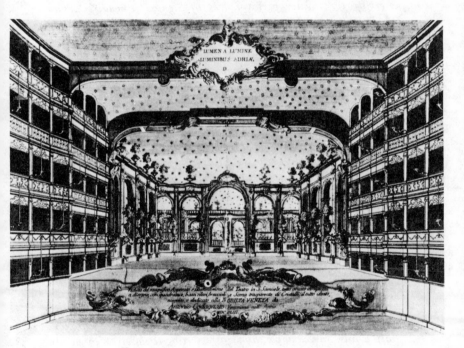

Ill. 74: Gabriel Bella: Veduta del magnifico apparato e illuminazione del Teatro in San Samuele totto oranto di Specchi

"Signor Grimani sent me to the musician to make the necessary changes in this opera, in part to shorten the drama, in part also to alter the position and the character of the arias to suit the singers and the composer. So I visited Don Vivaldi and had myself announced on instructions of His Excellency Grimaldi. I found him surrounded by music, the breviary in his hand. He got up, made the sign of the cross minutely, put the breviary aside and paid me the usual compliment: 'What is the reason for giving me the pleasure of seeing you?' 'His Excellency Grimaldi has commissioned me to make the changes in the opera for the next season which you consider necessary. I came here to see what your wishes are.' 'Oh, oh, you have been entrusted with the changes in the opera "Griselda"? Signor Lalli is apparently no longer serving the theater performances of Signor Grimaldi?' 'Signor Lalli is quite old and will always profit from the introductory dedications and the sale of the librettos which I am not concerned with. I will have the pleasure of occupying myself with a job which will surely give me pleasure, and I will have the honor to begin on instructions by Signor Vivaldi.' (The priest takes up his breviary again, repeats the sign of the cross and does not reply.) So I said: 'I did not want to disturb you during your religious exercises; I will better return at another time.' 'I know well that you have a talent for writing. I have seen your "Belisar" which gave me much pleasure, but there seems to be some difference: one may be able to write a tragedy, an epic poem, if you wish, and not succeed in doing a musical quatrain.' 'Please let me see your drama.' 'Yes, yes, I will do so; where is that Griselda hiding? She was here . . . Deus in adjutorium meum intende. Domine . . . Domine . . . she was here just now. Domine ad adjuvandum . . . Oh, here she is. You see, this scene between Gualterio and Griselda; it is an interesting scene, a moving one. The author put an emotional aria at the end, but Signorina Giraud does not like yearning songs, she prefers an expressive piece, excitement, an aria expressing passion in various ways, by broken-off words, for example, by sighs asserting themselves, by action and motion — I do not know if you understand me.' 'Yes, I understand very well; incidentally, I had the honor of hearing Signorina Giraud; I know that her voice is not very strong. . .' 'What do you say, sir; you are insulting my pupil? She is good for

162

everything, she sings everything.' 'Yes, sir, you are right. Just
give me the libretto and let me take care of it.' 'No, I cannot
give it away. I need it, I am in a hurry.' 'Just for that reason, if
you are in a hurry, let me have it for a moment, and I will satisfy
you immediately.' 'Immediately?' 'Yes, on the spot.'

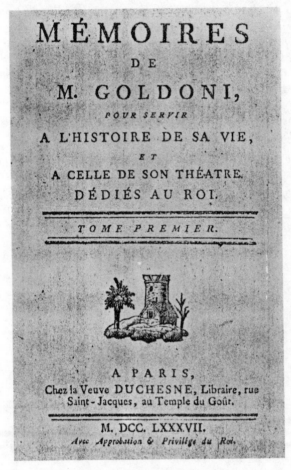

Ill. 75: Title page of the first edition of Goldoni:
Mémoires

"The priest made fun of me, gave me the drama, paper and writing untensils, returned to his breviary and recited his psalms and his hymns, while walking back and forth. I glanced over the scene which I already knew; I refreshed my memory as to what the musician wanted; and in less than 15 minutes I wrote down an aria in eight lines, divided in two sections. I called my priest over and showed him my work. Vivaldi read it; his face relaxed, as he reread it; he uttered loud cries of joy, threw his prayer-book to the floor and called Signorina Giraud. She came, and he told her: 'Oh, here we have a rare person, an excellent poet; read this aria; this gentleman has just written it, without moving away, in less than 15 minutes.' He returned to me: 'Oh, sir, I beg your pardon,' and he embraced me and insisted that he will never take another poet but me.

"He entrusted me with the drama, asked for some changes; he was always satisfied with me, and the opera was very successful.

"This is the way I was introduced to the opera, the comedy and the intermediary pieces which were the presursors of the Italian comic opera."

The year of crisis 1737

We are well informed about the events of this period through the correspondence between Vivaldi and the Marchese Bentivoglio which has already been mentioned frequently. Six letters were published in 1871 by F. Steffani, one in 1938 by F. Vatielli, another in 1955 by Pincherle. Research by Adriano Cavicchi resulted in 1967 in five more letters being found as well as all the replies by Bentivoglio in the State Archive of Ferrara and also five letters which closely touch upon the world of opera, as it existed in those times. This number can be augmented by one more letter which Lino Moretti imparted to the Vivaldi congress of Venice in 1978 (reprinted in: Antonio Vivaldi da Venezia all'Europa, Milano 1978, pp. 26–27).

(The preceding chapter follows to a large extent those letters made public by Cavicchi in the NRMI 1969/45–79).

At the end of the year 1736, Vivaldi had reached the peak of his career as opera composer and as impresario. In October 1736, a society made up of the nobility in Ferrara under the leadership of Bentivoglio commissioned the Abate Giuseppe Maria Bollani with the production of two operas for the forthcoming carnival. Bollani, a relative of Bentivoglio, went to see Vivaldi in Venice for discussions. The selection of Vivaldi may have had to do with the wedding of Francesco Stefano, Duke of Lorraine, to Maria Theresa of Habsburg which was celebrated in grand style with a serenade containing many movements by anonymous masters whose music originated perhaps largely with the "maestro di cappella" of the Duke and may have been conducted by him.

165

Bollani meant to get in touch also with "Signora Giró," in order to win her participation for the performances in Ferrara.

The composer answered on November 3, 1736 in the most exquisitely polite fashion:

". . . my poor pen would not suffice to express my thanks properly."

However, he began cautiously to take away the job as impresario from Bollani:

". . . I had followed no other goal in this matter than to show you my most humble respect and to create a perfect theatre. However, I assure Your Excellency that we succeeded in putting together a company, as has not, I hope, been seen during the carnival season on the stage of Ferrara in many years."

Now he got started with all of his business acumen and made calculations for his patron to the effect that for his sake he worked at the fee of a copyist.

"After having refused to write the third opera of San Cassiano for 90 zecchini, since they had to concede to me my customary fee of 100 zecchini, Ferrara will after all have two operas which will seem to have been made expressly for this occasion, since they were both arranged and completed in my own hand at a cost of only 6 zecchini for each opera which is the payment of a copyist."

He regretted that an urgent job for San Cassiano prevented him from coming to Ferrara.

"In any case, I will be at the feet of Your Excellency by the end of the carnival, if I can make it possible."

He used the same obsequious tone in representing the singer:

"Signorina Anna Giró expresses to Your Excellency her most humble respect, and since she is pleased to offer her imperfections in Ferrara, she also asks that you extend your strongest protection to her."

166

This was the style used by a composer intent on being successful in his correspondence with his "protettore" during the 18th century.

On November 24, 1736, Vivaldi informed his patron:

". . . I have decided to rewrite all recitatives and give the singers very many of my arias. The first act is already done, and all the singers will know their parts before leaving Venice."
(This has to do with a revision of an opera by Hasse.)

At the same time he said:

". . . that the Signor Impresario is about to miss the contract of Signora Mancini. . .,"

in which statement he was pointing at his own great experience in operatic dealings as compared with Bollani's.

On December 26, 1736, the information followed that Act 1 of "Alessandro nelle Indie" (also by Hasse) had already been given to the copyist; there were some changes in the libretto which he submitted. Then he again attacked Bollani:

"It seems that this is the year of impresarios with little experience. They are all like that, at San Cassiano, at San Angelo and also those in Brescia. I am not mentioning those in Ferrara."

On December 29, 1736, Vivaldi wrote a letter full of complaints about the miserly Bollani who wanted to pay so little that the expenses of the copyists were barely covered. He also constantly wanted other works.

"This man has no idea of the business of an impresario; he does not know where to spend and where to save money."

Bentivoglio answered on December 30, 1736 in part:

"I also believe that this is the year of the inexperienced impresarios."

167

Ill. 77: Canaletto (1697–1768): Venice, Ca'Rezzonico,
il Canale Grande visto da San Vito

He was asked for his intervention in matters of money:

"Your Excellency,
"In performance of my duty, I am sending to Signor Bertelli the
third act, so that it is handed over to you, and I assume that you
have already received the second act which I sent to you last
Saturday. I want to ask Your Excellency the favor to use your
authority to have the Signor Impresario pay at once to Signori-
na Girò the 6 zecchini as well as the 20 lire for the copyist
which I am rightfully entitled to. I feel that the opera is long,
and I was sure that an opera of four hours was not suitable for
Ferrara. By composing the recitatives, I cut it down forcibly. But
this Lanzetti prevented me on orders of the impresario . . .
Venice, January 2, 1737   *Antonio Vivaldi"*
(Lanzetti was a Venetian impresario to whom Bollani had turned.)

Vivaldi reported about performances in Verona:

Ill. 76: Canaletto (1697–1768): Venice, Il Bacino di San Marco visto dalla Punta della Giudecca

"We have [up to now] only given six performances; after the accounting I expect not to lose; but rather — if God favors us with good weather until the end — a profit is quite assured and perhaps not just a small one."

This was written in a letter from Verona of May 3, 1737, in which he gave some advice which lets us understand a little his business practices.

"This is, however, not possible to do during the carnival, since the dances alone, for which I can in summer demand a price to be determined by me, would cost me 700 luigi during the carnival. In similar cases I am a free agent, and I am paying out of my own pocket, not with borrowed money."

He had to fight for months with prima ballerina Coluzzi who had broken her contract and escaped from her father, in order to marry the dancer Pompeati.

". . . By nature a very bad person, capable of any nonsense and any peculiarity."

Toward the end of the year, bad luck befell him, and he wrote on November 16, 1737:

"Your Excellency,

"After so many obstructions and troubles, the opera in Ferrara is ruined. Today Monsignore, the Apostolic Nuncio, summoned me and decided in the name of His Eminence for me not to come to Ferrara to perform the opera. The reason is that I am a priest without reading mass and that I have an "amicizia" [friendship, affair] with the singer Girò. After my being hit so hard, Your Excellency can imagine my condition; I am carrying on my shoulders the load of the contracts for 600 ducats which were signed for this opera, and at this time I have advanced more than 100 zecchini. It is not possible to perform the opera without Girò, since I cannot find a similar primadonna. To perform the opera without me is not possible, since I cannot entrust such a large amount of money to strange hands. On the other hand, I am committed by the contracts which results in a sea of disasters. What makes me especially sad is the fact that His Eminence Ruffo attached a taint to these poor girls which the world never gave them.

"Fourteen years ago, we traveled together to most cities in Europe, and everywhere their manners were admired, and I can say the same about Ferrara. They go to confession and communion every week. . .

"In short, everything happens because of my illness, and these girls take good care of me, because they are informed about all my troubles.

"These are truths known nearly all over Europe. So I am turning to the goodwill of Your Excellency, so that you are kind enough to inform also His Eminence Ruffo. . ."

Cardinal Ruffo must have felt like a rock during a time of moral decay, and Vivaldi's life and activity as an impresario must have been for a long time a thorn in his side. Since Ferrara belonged to the territory of the Papal States of that period, he had authority even over a private

EMIN.ᵐᵉ ET REV.ᵐᵉ PRIN.ᵖᵉ
THOMÆ RUFO S.R.E. PRESBYTERO CARDINALI
TIT. S. MARIÆ TRANSTYBERIM
ET EPISCOPO FERRARIENSI.

Ill. 78: Cardinal Tommaso Ruffo

theatre undertaking. His action must be understood as part of his general efforts to reform the lives of clergymen. Ruffo issued on January 8, 1738 an "Editto in occasione del Carnevale" which reads in part:

"We order and enact specifically for all clergymen of any office, grade and position, whether secular priests or belonging to an order of this city and diocese who live here in any manner, that they remember the instructions of the holy laws, councils and apostolic constitutions, to refrain entirely from masquerading, from watching tightrope dancers and charlatans, from spending their time on the square and the corso and from taking indecent walks or taking part in any offensive dissoluteness of similar kind, especially participating in any way in balls, festivities, banquets on penalty of 50 scudi for each above-mentioned incident. . ."

Bentivoglio went at once to Ruffo to intervene, but in vain. Ruffo remained firm.

"He also assured me that he would remain firm in this decision, even if he received an order from the Pope to countermand it. He would rather lose the seat of the Archbishop than change his opinion, since he believes he had to act this way."
(Letter from Bentivoglio to Vivaldi of November 20, 1737)

He tried to salvage his opera performances for Ferrara, proposed to the composer to entrust the enterprise to a Signor Picchi, since Abate Bollani also could not, under the new conditions, be involved in the theatre any longer.

But Vivaldi had already accepted the unavoidable.

"God wants it this way, I cannot add anything else for Your Excellency."

he said in another letter of "23 9mbre 1737" (November 23, 1737). He continued:

"His Eminence Ruffo is not interested in the fact that I played in Rome and even twice in the private apartments of the Pope himself. He creates this obstacle, and I must accept it."

He adds:

"I never play in the orchestra, except for the first evening, because I do not consider it proper to practise the profession of an orchestra musician. I never reside in the [same] house as the sisters Girò. The evil tongues can say what they wish; Your Excellency knows that there is in Venice my own house for which I pay 200 ducats and another one, very far from mine, which belongs to the Girò's."

At that moment, in June 1738, Cardinal Ruffo unexpectedly resigned from his office as Archbishop of Ferrara. Whether the affair Vivaldi had anything to do with it? In any case, the probability exists that his rigid attitude, in other matters as well, may have resulted in an untenable position opposite the Pope. Illness can hardly have been the cause, since Ruffo died as late as 1753 at the age of 89.

Now that the road to Ferrara was open again for Vivaldi, he resumed the correspondence with Bentivoglio in November 1738, and "Siroe" and "Farnace" were prepared, although without the personal participation of Vivaldi. The fact that the libretto printed in Ferrara for "Siroe" is dedicated to the papal legate Agapito Mosca is not without a certain piquancy.

However, "Siroe" had a poor reception in Ferrara, and Vivaldi wrote a (last) letter to Bentivoglio:

> *"My reputation in Ferrara has suffered so badly that they now refuse to use "Farnace" as their second opera which was specially written for this company according to the contract with Mauro. My greatest offense is that they condemn my recitatives. Considering my name and reputation all over Europe and having composed 94 operas, I cannot stand any more such inconveniences."*

He complained about the poor harpsichord playing of the recitatives of the opera and was convinced that all this would not have happened if he had been present in Ferrara. Completely broken, he concluded:

> *"Your Excellency, I am desperate, I cannot bear it that such an ignorant person puts his fortune above the destruction of my poor name. I beg you for the mercy of God not to abandon me...*
> *"The fullest protection by Your Excellency is my only consolation in this situation, and while kissing your hands with tears in my eyes, I remain,*

> *Venice, January 2, 1739*   *Antonio Vivaldi"*

Conclusion in Venice

Once more fame from abroad spread over Vivaldi and his native city Venice. Ferdinand of Bavaria, the brother of the reigning Elector, visited Venice in 1739/40, and his special request was to see a performance at the Ospedale della Pietà. Vivaldi performed his dramatic cantata "Mopso," an "egloga pescatoria a cinque voci" which received great applause, and he was the recipient of great honors and rich gifts on this occasion.

On December 19, 1739, Prince Ferdinand-Christian, the son of the King of Poland and Elector of Saxony, arrived in Venice for a long sojourn. Of course, a visit to Vivaldi's institution was on the program, and the concert took place on March 21, 1740. A precious bound volume at the Dresden State Library contains the following:

> "Concerti con molti Istromenti Suonati dalle Figlie del Pio Ospitale della Pietà avanti Sua Altezza Reale Il Serenissimo Federico Cristiano Prencipe Reale di Polonia et Elettorale di Sassonia. Musica di D. Antonio Vivaldi Maestro de Concerti dell' Ospitale Sudetto. In Venezia nell'anno 1740"

It seemed that nothing had changed in the life of the composer, but deeper shadows began to fall over his life than the affair with Ruffo which affected the composer severely, especially in financial terms. De Brosses who had become close to the composer in August 1739 said in a letter of August 29:

> "I was very much surprised to find that he is not as much appreciated here as he deserves. Here everything follows the fashion and music from the previous year does not reap any profit; his works have been heard for too long a time."

Venice had gradually tired of Vivaldi's compositions which had not changed much over the last 30 years. At the Ospedale, there was a chance to learn about newer

Ill. 79: Francesco Guardi (1712–1793): Venice, Il Rio dei Mendicanti a Venezia

works by other composers; in the cashbooks, expenses were listed like the one of January 16, 1735 for Tartini's Sonatas, Op. 1 and on October 10, 1741, 72 lire were paid "per musica di Parigi [Paris]," proof that efforts were continuously made not to lose contact with the newest musical creations.

175

With the expression "profit" de Brosses hinted at the operas, and the last letter of Vivaldi proves that one began to look critically at his dramatic productions. In this connection two judgments which colleagues made who were exclusively writing instrumental music are of interest. Quantz did not mention Vivaldi by name, but there is no doubt that the remarks were meant for him:

> "Two famous violinists from Lombardy who, about thirty years ago and not far apart from each other, began getting better known, have contributed considerably in this respect. The first one was lively, rich in invention, and he filled half the world with his concertos. Even though Torelli and, later on, Corelli had made a start in this field, he created, together with Albinoni, a better form and produced good examples of them. Just as Corelli with his twelve solos, he reaped general approval through them. In the end he lapsed into carelessness and presumptuousness in composing and playing, all caused by his composing too much and every day, and especially by his starting to produce theatrical vocal music. As a result, his last concertos did not earn as much applause as his earlier ones."
> (Versuch einer Anweisung. . . XVIII. Hauptstück, 58§)

Tartini examined problems of dramatic compositions and their relation to instrumental music and mentioned Vivaldi in this connection:

> "These two genres are so different from each other that what is right for one, cannot be proper for the other. Everybody has to limit himself to his own talent. I have been asked to compose for the Venetian theatre, but I never wanted to, since I know that a throat is no fingerboard. Vivaldi wanted to work in both fields, was always booed in the one, while having very great success in the other."
> (Antonio Capri, G. Tartini, p. 78)

Tartini goes too far here, or he prejudges Vivaldi as an opera composer by looking at one particular case. To be booed, did not necessarily mean a qualitative judgment, if one considers the condition of the theatre during the 18th century. It is also hard to believe that an unsuccessful composer wrote about fifty operas, just to have them all booed, or rather that booed operas make it possible for a composer to have a successful opera career.

Equally, Goldoni's opinion about the "average composer" does not reflect the judgment of his contemporaries. When he wrote his "Mémoires," Vivaldi was practically forgotten, and the evolution of music had passed him by.

The observation made by de Brosses carries much weight, even if some of these judgments must be rejected or corrected. In the aftermath of the catastrophe of Ferrara, Vivaldi must have come to the conclusion around 1739/40 to leave his ungrateful native city and seek his fortune once more abroad.

For some time, Vivaldi had followed with concern the political development in Italy and the gradual decline of the former power of Venice, and this shows in a document which is deeply moving in its straightforward language. This is the dedication of the opera "Adelaide" in 1735 to the "Capitano" and "Vice Podestà" Antonio Grimani:

"It was equally fitting to dedicate this drama to a patrician in Venice, since the historical period from which the story dates, must displease any good Italian who is not, like so many nowadays, an enemy of his nation. It reminds him how poor Italy declined after the last Italian kings were driven out, only to become unable under foreign domination to extricate itself from such regrettable misfortune. The glorious republic of Venice is at least to some extent a consolation, where from the foundation up to our days the Italian freedom which God may preserve to the end of time has been maintained . . ."

Ill. 80: Andrea del Verrocchio (1435–1488):
Monumento a Bartolommeo Colleoni (1400–1475)

Death in Vienna

We do not know when Vivaldi left Venice and in which direction he went from there. He sold concertos to the Ospedale, probably to raise funds for his journey. In its meeting of April 29, 1740, the board of managers was occupied with the following question:

"*April 29, 1740*

"*Since it is necessary that our ensemble retain concertos for Organ and other instruments, in order to keep the above-mentioned ensemble in its usual good shape, and also because, when the Rev. Signor Vivaldi will leave this city, it so happens that he has prepared a certain number of concertos and it will be necessary to make a clear purchase of these:*

"*So it has been decided that the directors of church and institution are given the authority, assuming they seriously can take them over, to make the purchase at one zecchino for each concerto from our account, and the matter is then correct.*

Abstentions	3	
No votes	3	*rejected*"
Yes votes	4	

However, some invoices from this period have survived, and he actually received:

on April 27:	15 ducats and 13 lire for 3 concertos and 1 sinfonia,
on May 12:	70 ducats and 23 lire for 20 concertos,
on August 28:	1 ducat each for "un molta portione di concerti."

They apparently paid less every time, and Vivaldi had to be satisfied to get rid of the scores which would only have burdened his baggage.

Ill. 81: Receipt for 12 Hungarian Guilders, made out to the Count Collalto for a considerable number of works, possibly identical with a Sinfonia and 15 Concerti from the repertoire of the orchestra of the castle of Brtnice in Moravia. It is the last existing document by Vivaldi, written one month before his death.

He departed at the earliest during the first days of September 1740 and possibly went first to Graz where Anna Giraud had sung several times during 1739/40 under the impresarios Angelo and Pietro Mingotti, among other works in the Vivaldi operas "Rosmira" and "Catone in Utica."

His old patron Charles VI., whose favor he may have counted on, had died on October 20, presumably at the time Vivaldi arrived in Vienna. The beginning of the war of succession was not conducive to a new profitable start. Perhaps Vivaldi had planned to look in the direction of Prague and Dresden, or illness prevented him from continuing his journey. In any case, the last document signed by the master is dated June 26, 1741; it is a receipt confirming the sale of concertos to the Count Vinciguerra of Collalto. Possibly these were the works belonging to the repertoire of the court orchestra of Brtnice in Moravia which are now preserved in Brno (Brünn).

Vivaldi died in Vienna on July 28, 1741 and was buried the same day. Even the day and place of his death were unknown for a long time; occasionally, the year 1743 can still be found listed which was previously assumed to be the correct one. Rudolfo Gallo was prompted in 1938 by a passage in the handwritten "Commemoriali Gradenigo" (Venice, Museo Correr, II cap. 36) (see under "after 1741" in the introductory chapter) and found in Vienna

Ill. 82: Notations in the register of deaths of the Metropolitpfarramt (Metropolitan Church Office) of the Cathedral of St. Stephan, Vienna, Tomo 23, Fol 63

181

the two following entries in the register of deaths and also in the account book of St. Stephan:

> "28. Dito (July 1741)
>
> "The Rev. Antonj Vivaldi, secular priest in Satlerisch house near the Karner Thor, in the Spitaller gottsacker (cemetery), Kleingleuth (small pealing of bells)"
>
> (Vienna, Dom- und Metropolitanpfarramt St. Stephan, Death Register, Tomo 23, Fol. 63)

> "Conduct Vivaldi
>
> July 28
>
> "The Rev. Antonj Vivaldi, secular priest, has been examined at the Satlerisch house near the Karner Thor, [died of] internal gangrene, 60 years old, in the Spitaller gottsacker.

Small pealing of bells	2.36
Messrs. Curates	3.00
Shroud	2.15
Parish picture (?, Pfarrbild)	.30
Burial place	2.00
Untertaker and sacristan	1.15
Sexton	.30
6 pallbearers with cloaks	4.30
6 lanterns	2.00
6 boys in habit	.54
Bier	.15
Pelican"	19.48

(Vienna, Dom- und Metropolitanpfarramt St. Stephan, Death Register, Tomo 23, Fol. 63)

Based on a passage in the "Wiener Diarium" of August 2, 1741, the exact date of Vivaldi's death could be determined:

The house where Vivaldi died was torn down in 1873; it was located at the corner of Kärntnerstrasse and Sattlergässchen, where the "Kurier-Eck" is now situated. The cemetery was also closed.

Ill. 83: Engraving of Salomon Kleiner, 1737: Bürgerspitals- oder Armensündergottesacker (Cemetery of the Municipal Hospital or of the condemned criminals) in Vienna. In the background the Karlskirche

Survival through his works

Information dealing with Vivaldi's works during the decades following his death is very meager. In 1752, the English organist Charles Avison published an "Essay on Musical Expression" in London, where the composers Vivaldi, Tessarini, Alberti and Locatelli are mentioned as a group:

". . . whose Compositions being equally defective in various Harmony and true Invention, are only a fit Amusement for Children, nor indeed for these, if ever they are intended to be led to a just Taste in Music." (p. 39)

During the following year, an opposite voice was heard; Dr. William Hayes, professor of music at Oxford University, had an anonymous pamphlet printed, "Remarks on Mr. Avison's Essay on Musical Expression" (London 1753). He writes about the first group listed by Avison (p. 40):

"In Truth their Style is such, as I would not by any Means recommend; and yet I think Vivaldi has so much greater Merit than the rest, that he is worthy of some Distinction. Admitting therefore the same kind of Levity and Manner to be in his Compositions with those of Tessarini, etc., yet an essential Difference must still be allowed between the former and the latter; in as much as an Original is certainly preferable to a servile, mean copy."

Charles-Henri Blainville (1711–c. 1777) also had high esteem for Vivaldi. In his booklet "L'Esprit de l'art musical, ou Réflections sur la musique et ses différentes parties," which Hiller translated into German in his "Nachrichten" (1767/308), he mentioned Vivaldi and his "Spring" concerto next to Locatelli and remarked:

"The composer presents himself equally in the other Seasons, with as happy ideas, as a skillful painter. In any case, it is the best we have of its kind."

184

There were still occasional performances or references strangely referring nearly always to the "Spring" concerto from The Seasons. During the last year of the master's life, Pierre Gaviniès played, at the age of 13, this concerto at the "Concert spirituel" on All Saints' Day and received much applause. In 1766, Michel Corrette arranged the "Spring" concerto, making of it a motet "Laudate Dominum" for large chorus. Even the belated appreciation of Vivaldi by Auge Goudar in his pamphlet "De Venise, Remarque sur la musique et sur la danse" (1773) refers exclusively to The Seasons. Finally, Jean-Jacques Rousseau made in 1775 an arrangement of this concerto for flute solo (!), and Michel Corrette published in 1782 his "Art de se perfectionner dans le violon. . .," for which he took seven pages of examples from the opera VII—IX, most of them from The Seasons. In 1798, Jean-Baptiste Cartier was last, using in his "L'Art du violin" a Largo taken from the violin sonata in g minor, Op. V no. 6.

Thus, Vivaldi had disappeared from sight for good. In addition to the musicologist Bettinelli, quoted in the introductory chapter, numerous other authors, as Arteaga (1785), Perotti (1812), Bertini (1814/15), Majer (1821), Tipaldo (1834/45) and Canal (1847), could be quoted, to whom the name Vivaldi is unknown or who were only aware of some more or less trivial anecdotes about him, e.g. Count Grégoire Orloff who published a pamphlet "Essai sur l'histoire de la musique" (Paris 1822).

Vivaldi was only rediscovered when a manuscript was found during the preparation for a Bach Gesamtausgabe, "XII Concerti di Vivaldi, elaborati di J. S. Bach" with the notation "J. E. Bach, Lips. 1739." A relative of Bach, Johann Ernst Bach who was a St. Thomas graduate and for a time a student of Bach, had written it in Leipzig. It was published in 1851, and thus the world of music was faced with the strange phenomenon of the arrangements after Vivaldi by Bach, the importance of which Nikolaus

Forkel properly recognized. The interest shown by Hilgenfeldt (1850), Rühlmann (1867), Spitta (1873/80) and Waldersee (1885) was mainly directed at Bach, to be sure; but their investigations also unearthed works by Vivaldi which were hardly known up to that time. Arnold Schering (1905) and Wilhelm Fischer (in the Adler Handbook 1924) later saw Vivaldi in connection with the continuing development of music and recognized his importance through the works printed in Vivaldi's lifetime, for which Wilhelm Altmann had prepared a catalogue in 1922. Looking back today, a sentence by Schering, printed in 1905, appears almost grotesque:

> *"Does no concert management wish to try whether one of these beautiful concertos has the capacity for survival?"* (p. 60)

However, critics and audiences had to be led up the garden path first, before considering Vivaldi as a master whose works were worthy of being listened to. Fritz Kreisler has taken care of this matter thoroughly when he came forward in 1906 with his Vivaldi hoax which was just part of a series of hyphenated compositions. Vivaldi was suddenly popular, and the editorial efforts of Moffat and Nachèz were ready to start.

This was the situation, as it stood up to 1924, when, in the fall of that year, an impoverished Salesian monastery turned to the National Library in Turin with the request for an expert opinion, in order to. enable them to make an emergency sale of a large collection of musical manuscripts. The expert, Prof. Alberto Gentili, did not believe his eyes when he had before him 97 heavy volumes bound in pigskin, of which 14 contained works by Vivaldi which were up to that time unknown, among them church music and operas. The monastery had inherited these volumes from the estate of a Count Durazzo who died without succession. Gentili found a sponsor in the person of the banking authority Roberto Foà who bought these treasures and gave them to the National Library in

J. COMTE DE DURAZZO
Noble Genois
Ambassadeur Imperial a Venise

Ill. 84: Conte Giacomo Durazzo (1717–1794). From:
Benincasa: Descrizione . . ., Parma 1784

Turin in memory of his son Mauro who had died at the age of ten.

In examining the find more closely, Gentili made an exciting discovery: the volumes were numbered by groups, but in some of the series the even volumes were missing, in others the odd ones. The assumption that the collection had once been divided within the family, was confirmed after a search of several years for a very last member of the Durazzo family, the details of which read like a detective story. (It has been retold, based on the oral description by Gentili, in Kolneder: Antonio Vivaldi, Wiesbaden 1965; English edition, London 1970, also using family documents by Gabriella Verona-Gentili, Le Collezioni Foà e Giordano della Bibl. Naz. di Torino, in: Accad. e Bibl. d'Italia, Rome 1964). The second half of the collection could also be put in safekeeping in the Turin library through the generosity of the textile merchant Filippo Giordano who purchased and donated it. He also had lost a son Renzo in infancy. Since April 30, 1930, both parts of the great collection are combined in Turin as Collezioni Mauro Foà e Renzo Giordano.

Musicologists and editors realized only gradually the treasures that had to be brought to the surface. In 1939, a Vivaldi Week was organized in Siena under the patronage of Conte Guido Chigi dei Saracini; but its impact was undone by the outbreak of the Second World War. Only after the end of the war, these efforts were successful: Angelo Ephrikian and Antonio Fanna started their complete edition in 1946 under the artistic editorship of Gian Francesco Malipiero which was (temporarily) completed only in 1968, and in 1948 the large Vivaldi volume by Marc Pincherle appeared which contained the thematic listing.

After the instrumental music and the sacred works were recovered, the question arose as to what place the operatic creations of Vivaldi were to fill or could fill in our repertoire. The first modern performance was an experiment with the opera "Olimpiade" in Siena on September 19, 1939. However, Alfredo Casella, the artistic consultant of the Vivaldi Week, as well as the editor Virgilio Mortari have commented in an interesting manner. Casella said:

"The selection of 'Olimpiade' from the numerous operas by Vivaldi resting in the National Library of Turin was mainly influenced by the superior quality of the beautiful libretto of Metastasio (which was used also by other composers, among them Caldara, Jommelli, Pérez and finally Pergolesi), but also by the unique beauty of the music. Nevertheless, the work needed patient work in editing, especially because of the necessity to shorten to the absolute minimum the recitatives which modern audiences surely would not listen to. Since, in addition, some important pieces were missing, these were taken from another opera by Vivaldi, 'Dorilla,' which was also performed at the Teatro San Angelo in Venice during the same year (1734). The Turin score of 'Dorilla' contains the remark 'three acts with sinfonia and choruses which sing and dance;' the work is much richer in ensembles than 'Olimpiade,' especially in choruses and dances. For this reason, what was missing in 'Olimpiade' was borrowed from this opera, in the knowledge that nothing was done that the masters of that period had not been doing continually. (In my research in the Turin National Library, I found one identical aria in four different operas by Vivaldi!)."

(Alfredo Casella, Come sono state scelte ed elaborate le Musique della "Settiamana" in Antonio Vivaldi, Note e Documenti sulla via e sulle opere, Siena 1939.)

Mortari said the following about how he proceeded with the editing:

"The person charged with the arrangement and editing has the duty to perform a stylistically perfect job which is exact in every detail and humble without demanding from the public that it suffer strictness and conventions which are without doubt intolerable today. Therefore, the harpsichord which accompanies the recitatives was eliminated in all arias (!) where the orchestration represents the harmony with well-sounding result. Not all pieces in the original score were of equal importance, and it was considered necessary to make cuts, transpositions in the order of numbers and exchanges. The overlong recitatives were reduced to the shortest possible length, since a recitative which extends beyond a certain length, becomes

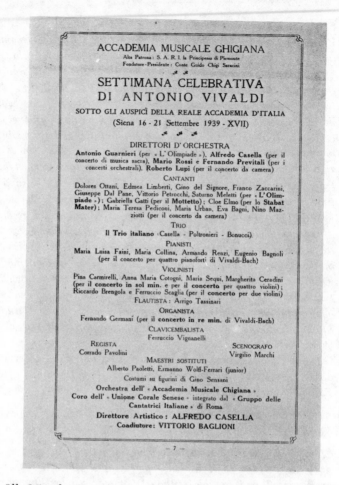

ACCADEMIA MUSICALE GHIGIANA
Alta Patrona: S. A. R. I. la Principessa di Piemonte
Fondatore - Presidente: Conte Guido Chigi Saracini

SETTIMANA CELEBRATIVA
DI ANTONIO VIVALDI

SOTTO GLI AUSPICÎ DELLA REALE ACCADEMIA D'ITALIA
(Siena 16 - 21 Settembre 1939 - XVII)

DIRETTORI D' ORCHESTRA
Antonio Guarnieri (per « L' Olimpiade »), **Alfredo Casella** (per il
concerto di musica sacra), **Mario Rossi** e **Fernando Previtali** (per i
concerti orchestrali), **Roberto Lupi** (per il concerto da camera)

CANTANTI
Dolores Ottani, Edmea Limberti, Gino del Signore, Franco Zaccarini,
Giuseppe Dal Pane, Vittorio Petrocchi, Saturno Meletti (per « **L'Olim-
piade** »); Gabriella Gatti (per il **Mottetto**); Cloe Elmo (per lo **Stabat
Mater**); Maria Teresa Pediconi, Maria Urban, Eva Bagni, Nino Maz-
ziotti (per il concerto da camera)

TRIO
Il Trio italiano (Casella - Poltronieri - Bonucci)

PIANISTI
Maria Luisa Faini, Maria Collina, Armando Renzi, Eugenio Bagnoli
(per il concerto per quattro pianoforti di Vivaldi-Bach)

VIOLINISTI
Pina Carmirelli, Anna Maria Cotogni, Maria Sequi, Margherita Ceradini
(per il **concerto in sol min.** e per il **concerto** per quattro violini);
Riccardo Brengola e Ferruccio Scaglia (per il **concerto** per due violini)

FLAUTISTA: Arrigo Tassinari

ORGANISTA
Fernando Germani (per il **concerto in re min.** di Vivaldi-Bach)

CLAVICEMBALISTA
Ferruccio Vignanelli

REGISTA
Corrado Pavolini

SCENOGRAFO
Virgilio Marchi

MAESTRI SOSTITUTI
Alberto Paoletti, Ermanno Wolff-Ferrari (junior)

Costumi su figurini di Gino Sensani

Orchestra dell' « Accademia Musicale Chigiana »
Coro dell' « Unione Corale Senese » integrato dal « Gruppo delle
Cantatrici Italiane » di Roma

Direttore Artistico: ALFREDO CASELLA
Coadiutore: VITTORIO BAGLIONI

— 7 —

*Ill. 85 a/b: Two programs of the Vivaldi Week, Siena,
September 16–21, 1939.*

an obstacle to the endurance of a modern listener. The strong
expressiveness of the music did not require any enriching of the
tone color of the original. The sound which is part of the style,
remained untouched in its function."
(Virgilio Mortari, "L'Olimpiade" e il Teatro musicale di Antonio
Vivaldi, in the same booklet)

190

TEMPIO DI S. FRANCESCO

Mercoledì 20 Settembre 1939 - XVII, alle ore 17

CONCERTO DI MUSICA SACRA

PER VOCI, CORO, ORGANO ED ORCHESTRA

1. CREDO per coro, organo ed archi.
   a) Credo in unum Deum ; b)
   c) Crucifixus ; d) Et resurrexit.

2. MOTTETTO per soprano, organo ed orchestra.
   a) O qui caeli - *b)* Recitativo - *c)* Rosa quae moritur -
   d) Alleluia.
   Soprano: GABRIELLA GATTI

3. STABAT MATER per contralto, organo ed archi.
   a) Staba mater dolorosa - *b)* Recitativo - *c)* Pro pec-
   catis suae - *d)* Eja mater - *e)* Fac, ut ardeat cor
   meum - *f)* Amen.
   Contralto: CLOE ELMO

4. GLORIA per due soprani, contralto, coro, organo ed orchestra.
   a) Gloria in excelsis Deo (coro) ;
   b) Et in terra pax hominibus (coro) ;
   c) Laudamus te (duetto per soprani) ;
   d) Gratias agimus tibi (coro) ;
   e) Propter magna gloria (coro) ;
   f) Domine Deus (soprano ed oboe solo) ;
   g) Domine Fili unigenite (coro) ;
   h) Domine Deus, Agnus Dei (contralto solo e coro) ;
   i) Qui tollis peccata mundi (coro) ;
   l) Qui sedes ad dexteram (contralto solo) ;
   m) Quoniam tu solus Sanctus (coro) ;
   n) Cum Sanctu Spiritu (coro).
   Soprani: MARIA TERESA PEDICONI ed EVA BAGNI
   Contralto: CLOE ELMO
   Oboe: FRANCO CARAMIA
   Coro: « UNIONE CORALE SENESE » integrato dal « *Gruppo
   delle Cantatrici Italiane* » di Roma
   Organista: FERRUCCIO VIGNANELLI
   Maestro del coro: VITTORIO BAGLIONI

DIRETTORE D'ORCHESTRA: **ALFREDO CASELLA**

N. B. - Il concerto sarà trasmesso dall' E. I. A. R.

— 15 —

In Paris, "La Fida Ninfa" was performed in full con-
formity with the score in 1958, but the work enjoyed
only moderate success. A review by Edgar Schall said
(Schweizerische Musikzeitung 1958/353):

> *"The modern opera lovers did no longer show sufficient interest in the totally undramatic "dramma pastorale" which had its first performance in Verona in 1732, even if the two female and four male singers did honor to the Italian schooling. The greatest admirers of Vivaldi were in the end restlessly moving in their seats, since during three hours really nothing happened on the stage. In order to preserve historic accuracy, all enlivening additions were strictly omitted. Only some very severe cuts would have helped to improve the enjoyment of the musical qualities."*

Another performance of "La Fida Ninfa" in Marseille in 1964 has been described by Jacques Lonchampt in his book "L'Opéra aujourd'hui;"

> *"In spite of his love for the work, Louis Ducreux was forced to cut the score by a good third, since in Vivaldi's day the composer as well as his public were less demanding than today. So long as the music was good, any libretto was sufficient, and the one by Scipio Maffei is at once extremely complicated and dramatically non-existent. . . We could have yawned, if it had not been for Vivaldi who wove arias of the purest melodic line and at the same time the moderate warmth of feeling over these unhappy events, with pages of noble greatness anticipating Gluck. There are ensembles full of picturesque drive, characteristic designs, interludes and ritornellos, very skillfully written and sometimes full of irony in which one recognizes his instrumental invention."* (p. 155)

These are the two extremes in trying to revive such works: tedium at an historically correct performance or interference, especially in the endless flow of recitatives, and salvaging of much beautiful music for the modern listener who suffers from a steadily shrinking repertoire. The record industry has so far avoided taking part in this attempt at rescue, although there is a continuous search for "novelties." Only during the most recent years have works like "Tito Manlio" and "Orlando furioso" appeared which indicate a change.

It should be mentioned that Vivaldi enjoys the greatest popularity among dancers. The rhythmic drive of his music

IN MEMORIA DI MAVRO FOÀ
I GENITORI

IN MEMORIA DI RENZO GIORDANO
I GENITORI

Ill. 86: Vignettes from the collections Foà and Giordano in the National Library, Turin representing Mauro Foà and Renzo Giordano

makes dancers move, in a way, by themselves. Having written much music with programmatic titles. Vivaldi's music facilitates the work of choreographers. To read in ballet reviews about Vivaldi interpretation implies mainly the physical motion in rendering his music.

193

It was actually a revelation to have the dancer Eva Campianu prove with the help of examples at the Vivaldi Colloquium in Bonn in March 1979 that dance steps reappear as rhythmic patterns in numerous concerto 'movements. This lets body motion be recognized as the immediate source of invention in the music of Vivaldi.

For Vivaldi research, it is of the greatest importance that Antonio Fanna, the editor of the complete Vivaldi edition, has put his entire archives at the disposal of the Fondazione Giorgio Cini in 1978. This will make it possible for this foundation which is located on the Isola San Giorgio in Venice to become to a much greater extent a center for all efforts dealing with the work and the person of the composer.

The circulation of the works of Vivaldi in the civilized world of his times is even nowadays having its full effect: not a year passes without some unknown compositions being found somewhere — far away from the centers of culture — in public libraries and private collections. Their acquaintance does not perhaps change our over-all picture of the master to a large extent, but it contributes to giving us an idea of the astonishing effectiveness of his work. Today, about fifty years after the discoveries in Turin, Vivaldi stands with his complete work covering all areas of musical creation at the center of our concert life, in chamber music, in radio and television broadcasts and, above all, in record productions.

In an article "Order of popularity among musicians . . ." (A.f.Mw. 1966/144), Albert Wellek has found that in the February 1966 issue of the Schwann catalogue which lists all commercially available recordings in U.S.A. every month, the "most established and most popular masters" appear in the following order:

Ill. 87: Francesco Guardi (1712–1793): Venice, San Giorgio Maggiore vista d'alla Giudecca

Mozart	Wagner
Bach	Tchaikovsky
Beethoven	Brahms
Haydn	Schubert
Vivaldi	Handel.

(In the November 1980 issue, there are nearly 8 columns of works by Vivaldi listed, compared to 8 1/2 columns of

Ill. 88: Francesco Guardi (1712—1793): Venice,
L'Isola San Giorgio

Haydn and 5 1/4 columns of Wagner, so that the popularity ratings appear to be unchanged after fourteen years.
The Translator.)

And in a record review (MQ 1961/566), Paul Henry
Lang observed that Vivaldi may have been a "Venetian
musical industrialist," but that he "was a poet of deep
emotion, insatiable in his quest for new horizons, and
above all a fiercely individual and original musical thinker."

Quotations in the original languages

Page 9
Joh. Seb. Bachs erste Versuche in der Composition waren wie alle erste Versuche mangelhaft. Ohne einigen Unterricht, durch welchen ihm ein Weg vorgezeichnet worden wäre, der ihn allmählig von Stufe zu Stufe hätte führen können, mußte er so wie alle diejenigen, die ohne Leitung eine solche Bahn betreten, anfänglich machen, wie es werden wollte. Auf dem Instrumente auf und ab laufen oder springen, beyde Hände dabey so voll nehmen, als die fünf Finger erlauben wollen, und dieses wilde Wesen so lange forttreiben, bis irgend ein Ruhepunkt zufälliger Weise erhascht wird, sind die Künste, welche alle Anfänger mit einander gemein haben. Sie können daher auch nur Fingercomponisten seyn (oder Clavier-Husaren, wie sie Bach in seinen spätern Jahren nannte) das heißt: sie müssen sich von ihren Fingern vormachen lassen, was sie schreiben sollen, anstatt daß sie den Fingern vorschreiben müßten, was sie spielen sollen. B a c h blieb aber nicht lange auf diesem Wege. Er fing bald an zu fühlen, daß es mit dem ewigen Laufen und Springen nicht ausgerichtet sey, daß Ordnung, Zusammenhang und Verhältniß in die Gedanken gebracht werden müsse, und daß man zur Erreichung solcher Zwecke irgend eine Art von Anleitung bedürfe. Als eine solche Anleitung dienten ihm die damals neu herausgekommenen Violinconcerte von V i v a l d i. Er hörte sie so häufig als vortreffliche Musikstücke rühmen, daß er dadurch auf den glücklichen Einfall kam, sie sämtlich für sein Clavier einzurichten. Er studirte die Führung der Gedanken, das Verhältniß derselben unter einander, die Abwechslungen

197

der Modulation und mancherley andere Dinge mehr. Die Umänderung der für die Violine eingerichteten, dem Clavier aber nicht angemessenen Gedanken und Passagen, lehrte ihn auch musikalisch denken, so daß er nach vollbrachter Arbeit seine Gedanken nicht mehr von seinen Fingern zu erwarten brauchte, sondern sie schon aus eigener Fantasie nehmen konnte.

Page 10

. . . zu trachten noch einige rare compositiones des Vivaldi zu erhalten und nechstens zu behendigen . . .

At that period in Pirna, I became for the first time acquainted with the violin concertos of Vivaldi. Being an entirely new kind of musical composition then, they made a deep impression upon me. I did not let the opportunity pass to collect quite a large number of them. The beautiful ritornelle of Vivaldi served me in in future years as an excellent model.

. . . gegen das ende spielte der vivaldi ein accompagnement solo, admirabel, woran er zuletzt eine phantasie anhing, die mich recht erschrecket, denn dergleichen ohnmöglich so jehmahls ist gespielt worden, noch kann gespiehlet werden, denn er kahm mit den Fingern nur einen strohhalm breit an den steg daß der bogen keinen plaz hatte, und das auf allen 4 saiten mit Fugen und einer geschwindigkeit die unglaublich ist . . .

Page 12

Le roi (Louis XV) demanda qu'on jouat Le Printemps de Vivaldi.

Per questo ho l'onore di carteggiare con nove Principi d'altezza, e girono le mie lettere per tutto l'Europa.

198

L'Abbate Antonio Vivaldi eccelentissimo Sonatore di Violino, detto il Prete Rosso, stimato compositore de concerti, guadagnò ai suoi giorni cinquantamille ducati, ma per sproporzionata prodigalità morì miserabile in Vienna.

Page 13
Die Originalwerke des Vivaldi gehören längst zu den musikalischen Seltenheiten, und deshalb möchte es gegenwärtig Schwierigkeiten haben, mit Bestimmtheit nachweisen zu wollen, aus welchem Opus seiner uns grösstentheils nur dem Titel nach bekannten Instrumentalwerke, J. S. Bach eine Auswahl für die vorliegenden Bearbeitungen getroffen hat.

Page 16
Il primo criterio al quale ci siamo attenuti è stato quello di presentare tutti gli aspetti della gigantesca figura del "Prete rosso", e cioè la musica teatrale, quella religiosa, e quella strumentale accanto all'altra cameristica.

Page 18
Dans le Largo de l'Hiver, Vivaldi témoigne de l'exceptionelle sensibilité qui est la sienne aux rythmes cosmiques des saisons.

Page 19
. . . essendo chiarissima et vera cosa che la musica ha la sua propria sede in questa città.

Page 20
Adi 6 Maggio 1678
Antonio Lucio figliolo del Sig.^{r} Gio.Batta quondam Agustin Vivaldi sonador et della Sig^{ra} Camilla figliola del Sig^r Camillo Calicchio sua consorte, nato li 4 marzo ultimo caduto qual'hebbe l'acqua in casa per pericolo di morte dalla comare allevatrice. Madama Margarita Veronese, hoggi fu portato alla Chiesa ricevé l'essorcismi

et agli Santissimi da me Giacomo Fanacieri Piovano a quali lo tene il Sig^r Antonio quondam Gerolamo Vecchio specier all'Insegna del Dose in Contrà.

Page 23

Adi 23 Aprile 1685

GI'Ill.mi et Ece.mi Signori Procuratori infrascritti cioè Gio. Battista Cornaro, Marco Ruzini, Giulio Giustinian, Alvise Mocenigo 4.to, Silvestro Valier, Ottaviano Marini, Zaccaria Vallaresso, Francesco Cornaro absenti l'ill.mi et ecc.mi Signori Procuratori Giovanni Pisani hanno terminato che siano accettati nella Cappella della Chiesa Ducale di San Marco per concerti li sottoscritti con hordinaria proviggione de ducati quindeci all'anno per cadauno e posti nel Libro de conformità da subito partecipare in simili occorrenza et sic est

Francesco Valletta per sonar la Viola da braccio con ducati quindeci.

Gio.Baptista Rossi per sonar il Violin con ducati quindeci.

Lodovico Vaccio per sonar il trombon con ducati quindeci.

De si   7
De non   —
Non sinceri 1

Page 26

Ellettione di Gio.Batta Vivaldi detto Rosetto per Maestro d'Instrumenti.

Page 34/35

Die Veneris decima octava mensis Septembris 1693 Venetii in Oratorio Patriarchalis Palatii . . . Ill. et Rev. mus D.D.Joannes Baduarius misericordia divina Patriarcha Venetiarum, Dalmatiaeque Primas Clericali Tonsura insignivet infrascriptes: . . . Antonius filius Jo.Bap.tae Vivaldi Ecclesiae S.Geminiani.

200

Page 36
A.D.Antonio Vivaldi Maestro di Choro e deve addì 17 Marzo a cassa d.decontadi a lui per suo honorario di mesi sei finiti ultimo febraio passato.

Maestri novi di Choro
Per ridur sempre più perfettionato il Choro e renderlo di maggior politia nell'armonia dello stesso in ordine à ciò che arricorda il Signor Gasparini nostro Maestro di Choro; Và parte che dalli Signori Deputati sopra il Choro siano eletti Maestri di Viola Violin, et Aboè con quella ricognitione alli stessi che sarà stimata propria, e di minor aggravio di questo pio loco, trattenendoli al servitio per quel tempo, che conosceranno necessario, e resti fermo quanto sarà da essi operato come fatto da questa Congregatine.

Page 37
Addì 17 agosto 1704
Continuando con frutto don Antonio Vivaldi Maestro di Violin delle figliole, e con assidua assistenza anco nell'insegnamento della Viola Inglese che però considerato da SS.EE. l'impiego dello stesso, si manda parte restino aggionti al solito suo honorario altri ducati quaranta all'anno per insegnar le Viole all'Inglese; così che in tutto siino ducati cento all'anno con che resti incorraggito nelle proprie incombenze, e per il frutto maggiore di esse figliole.

de si   n.9 ⎱
de no   n.1 ⎰ presa

Page 40
Il y a, à Venise, des couvents de femmes où ces dernières jouent de l'orgue, de différents instruments et chantent, si admirablement, que nulle part ailleurs dans le monde on ne trouverait des chants si doux et si harmonieux. Aussi vient-on de tout part à Venise avec

201

le désir de se nourrir de ces chants angéliques, surtout
de celui du couvent des Incurables.

La musique transcendante ici est celle des hôpitaux. Il
y en a quatre, tous composés de filles bâtardes ou
orphelines, et de celles que leurs parents ne sont pas
en état d'élever. Elles sont élevées aux dépens de l'Etat,
et on les exerce uniquement à exceller dans la musique.
Aussi chantent-elles comme des anges, et jouent du violon, de la flûte, de l'orgue, du hautbois, du violoncelle,
du basson; bref, il n'y a si gros instrument qui puisse
leur faire peur. Elles sont cloîtrées en façon de religieu-
ses. Ce sont elles seules qui exécutent, et chaque concert
est composé d'une quarantaine de filles. Je vous jure qu'
il n'y a rien de si plaisant que de voir une jeune et jolie
religieuse, en habit blanc, avec un bouquet de grenades
sur l'oreille, conduire l'orchestre et battre la mesure
avec toute la grâce et la précision imaginables. Leurs
voix sont adorables pour la tournure et la légèreté;
car on ne sait ici ce que c'est que rondeur et sons filés
à la française. La Zabetta, des Incurables, est surtout
étonnante par l'étendue de sa voix et les coups d'archet
qu'elle a dans le gosier. Pour moi, je ne fais aucun doute
qu'elle n'ait avalé le violon de Somis. C'est elle qui
enlève tous les suffrages, et ce serait vouloir se faire
assommer par la populace que d'égaler quelque autre
à elle. Mais écoutez, mes amis, je crois que personne ne
nous entend, et je vous dis à l'oreille que la Margarita,
des *Mendicanti*, la vaut bien et me plaît davantage.
Celui des quatre hôpitaux, où je vais le plus souvent, et
où je m'amuse le mieux, c'est l'hôpital de la Piété; c'est
aussi le premier pour la perfection des symphonies.
Quelle raideur d'exécution! C'est là seulement qu'on
entend ce premier coup d'archet, si faussement vanté
à l'Opéra de Paris. La Chiaretta serait sûrement le
premier violon de l'Italie, si l'Anna-Maria, des Hospi-
talettes, ne la surpassait encore.

202

Page 44

2. Juni 1715

Rileva questa Pia Congregatione dalla Supplica del
Reverendo Don Antonio Vivaldi Maestro di Violino
del Choro di questo Pio Locco, et dalla scrittuara delli
Signori Governatori Nostri Deputati al Choro ora letta,
le ben notte applicationi, e frutuose fatiche prestate dal
Medesimo, non solo nel educar le figlie nelli concerti di
suono, con frutto, e universale agradimento, mà anco le
vertuose compositioni in musica contribuite doppo l'
absenza del sudetto maestro Gasparini, di una Messa
intiera, un Vespero, un Oratorio, più di trenta Mottet-
ti et altre fatiche. Et conoscendo giusto la benignità di
questa Pia Congregatione di darlli testimonij di gratitu-
dine, e riconoscerllo in parte, per talli estraordinarie
fatiche. Sia preso che in agradimento delle medesime
sue applicantioni, et fatiche estraordinarie li sijno per
questa volta tanto esborsati da questa nostra Cassa ducati cinquanta: Et li serviranno anco di vivo stimolo per
sempre più contribuire e perfettionare maggiormente le
figlie di questo nostro Choro nelle vertuose cognitioni,
che si rendono tanto necessarie al Choro stesso, e per il
maggior decoro di questa nostra Chiesa.

non sincere	n.—	⎫
de no	n.2	⎬ presa
de si	n.10	⎭

Page 46

Sono venticinque anni che io non dico messa, ne mai più
la dirò, non per vieto o commando, comme si può informare Sua Eminenza, ma per la mia elezione, e ciò stante
un male che patisco 'a nativitate', pel quale io sto
oppresso. Appena ordinato, un anno o poco più ho
detto messa, e poi l'ho lasciata avendo dovuto tre
volte partir dall'altare senza terminarla a causa dello
stesso mio male.
Per questo io vivo quasi sempre in casa, e non esco che
in gondola o in carrozza, perchè non posso camminare

per male di petto ossia strezzeta di petto. Non v'è alcun cavaliere che mi chiami alla sua casa, nemmeno l'istesso nostro Principe, mentre tutti sono informati del mio difetto. Subito dopo il pranzo ordinariamente io posso andare, ma mai a piedi. Ecco la ragione per la quale non celebro messa.

Page 51

Alli dilettanti di musica

Il cortese compiacimento, che sin'hora avete donato alle mie debolezze, mi ha persuaso a studiare di compiacervi con un'Opera di Concerti Istrumentali. Confesso bene che se per il passato le mie composizioni oltre i loro difetti ànno ancora avuto il discapito della stampa, hora il loro maggior avantaggio sarà quello di essere scolpite dalla mano famosa di Monsieur Estienne Roger. Quest'è una ragione per la quale ho studiato di sattisfarvi con la stampa di Concerti e mi fa coraggio di presto presentarvi un'altra Muta di Concerti a 4. Concervatemi il vostro buon genio e vivete felici.

Page 56/57/58

Sire,

E invidiabile la fortuna delle adorazioni d'un cuore ossequioso, se incontrando in un qualche Sovrano Grande per Nascita, ma più Grande per Virtù, è sforzato ad essere sicuro dell'aggradimento de' suoi tributi, quali essi siano. Questa verità, che costrinse il mio intelletto a riflettere all'Eroico dell'animo di Vostra Maestà ben conosciuto dal Mondo tutto, mi diede tanta confidenza per offerire le mie umiliazioni, che non potè dalla giusta considerazione del mio niente essere in verun conto scemata. Non vi potea far maggiore la Sorte, inalzandovi ad un posto riguardevole e per Maestà, e per Potenza; ma la vostra Grandezza erasi resa poco utile, perché troppo lontana da chi era al basso. Voi Scendeste dal Trono, e l'umiltà tolse gl'impedimenti della Vostra Altezza per consolare chi tutto inchinato confessavasi indegno di nè pur baciare l'ultimo gradino del Vostro Soglio. Gradite dunque, o Gran Re, non l'offerta, che non ha proporzione col Vostr' Essere, ma 'l cuore che offerisce, perciocché se 'l cuor solo può dar prezzo a ciò ch'è vile, e peso a ciò ch'è mancante, non dovete rivolger l'occhio da questo qual si sia tributo, perche viene da un animo, che col più profondo ossequio si vanta che possi anch'io essere stimato, qual bramo di consagrarmi.

Di Vostra Maestà
Umilissimo Devotissimo Ossequiosissimo Servitore
Antonio Vivaldi

Page 62

Der Beginn dieses Orgelconzertes mit seinem gewaltigen Orgelpunkt auf D und seinem grossen Crescendo bot die Gelegenheit und reizte mich unwillkürlich, das Anwachsen und Aufsteigen der Tonmassen zu vergrößern und zu verlängern. Auch kam mir dieser langsam anschwellende D moll-Accord wie ein in weiter Ferne liegender, fast vergessener Vorläufer des Es dur-Accordes zu Beginn des "Rheingoldes" von R. Wagner vor. Die heutigen grossen Concertflügel geben die Möglichkeit, vom leisesten ppp bis zum gewaltigsten fff eine Steigerung zu machen. Mit Ausnahme der Einleitung, die um mehrere Takte gegenüber dem Originale vermehrt wurde, und der Cadenz (welche ad libitum ist) habe ich mich streng und genau an das Original gehalten, versuchend die Gewalt der Orgel durch breite Setzung zu imitieren . . .

Diese Cadenz habe ich dem stürmischen Charakter des Werkes angepasst. Das Titelbild giebt die Grundstimmung des Concertes "Sturm, finstere Wolken über das Firmament rasend, Blitz und Donner". Die Nationalzeitung in Berlin schrieb anläßlich eines meiner Concerte in Berlin: "Der Vortrag des W. F. Bach'schen Orgelconcertes machte auf uns den Eindruck eines großen Naturschauspieles. Man sah Berge wanken und den Sturm Bäume entwurzeln." Ich glaube hinzufügen zu können, dass ich dieses Orgelconcert des unglücklichen und unsteten W. F. Bach — vielleicht ein Spiegelbild seiner eigenen ruhelosen Seele — für den ersten, auf wahren Kunstwerth Anspruch machenden Vorläufer der grossartigen Sturmesphantasien von Beethoven, Wagner und Liszt halte.

Page 63

Nel libro sonvi regole di musica inclusive alcune osservazioni sul bene accompagnare alla spinetta et all'organo nelle chiese. Anche gli intendori quali il rev. Vivaldi che fa musica alla Pietà ne fanno l'elogio.

Page 64

Er wurde einsmals, auf Veranlassung des Königlichen Churprinzen von Sachsen genöthiget, bey einer Oper im Orchester, (ich weis nicht ob bey St. Chrisostomo oder St. Angelo) vermuthlich, weil damals die Tänze noch nicht so wie heut zu Tage in den Opern üblich waren, zwischen zweenen Acten, ein Violin-Concert zu spielen. Er nahm dazu eines aus dem F dur, mit Waldhörnern, von Vivaldi, welches diesen Unisono-Anfang hat:

Der letzte Satz dieses Concerts fängt sich so an:

In diesem letztern Satz fängt die Concertstimme mit einem cantabeln Solo an. Zuletzt aber hat sie eine lange Passagie von zwey und dreißigtheilen, die ganz in der Applicatur liegt (bei der man die Lage ständig ändern muß). Bey dieser Passagie suchten die Herren, aus denen das Orchester bestand, und welche alle Italiäner waren, durch Uebereilung des Accompagnements den Herrn Pisendel in Unordnung zu bringen. Er hingegen

206

e 130

Riva ad attendere c'era il clero di S.Marco con torce
ese e accompagnati dai musici che intonavano un
udate Dominum solennissimo opera dell'abate Vivaldi
la Pietà . . .

131/132

n il sollitto della loro attentione li Signori Governato-
Nostri Deputati alla Chiesa, e Choro nella loro scritura
a letta in esecuttione della parte questa Veneranda
ngregatione i luglio passato esibbiscono per Maestro
Concerti di questo nostro Choro il Reverendo D.An-
io Vivaldi professore di piena abbillita all'incomben-
stessa.

verà, presa che sia la parte il Maestro stesso somini-
re a questo nostre Figlie li conserti , e compositioni
ogni genere d'Instrumenti, e doverà pure prestarsi
la dovuta frequenza ad instruire le Figlie, che do-
anno valersi per renderle capaci della Maniera di ben
guirveli. E così pure sarà tenuto à render nella miglio-
maniera instruire nelle cognittioni di quei instrumenti
si esercittassero di queste nostre Figlie, e ne fossero
gniose. Et per sua Mercede doverà consegguire il
estro stesso ducati Cento conn.ti all'anno, giusto il
posto dalla Presente scrittura.

la mettà

non sincere	n.3	
de no	n.2	presa
de si	n.8	

ra gl'eccitamenti fatti da questa Pia Congregatione
carità delli Signori Governatori Deputati alla Chiesa,
horo, venendo con la loro scrittura hora letta rapre-
ata l'indespensabile necessità che ci sij almeno per
lche tempo in questo nostro Choro un Maestro di
loncello per ridurlo ad una perfetta armonia, e con-
o et tenendo l'incontro di valersi del Reverendo D.

ließ sich ihr Eilen nicht im geringsten anfechten, sondern erhielt jene, die ihm eine Grube graben wollten,
durch Stampfen mit den Füßen so feste im Takte, daß
sie alle beschämt wurden. Der Prinz hatte darüber eine
besondere Freude . . .

Page 67

Il fallut séjourner le 31 pour entendre Tartini, qui passe
communément pour le premier violon de l'Italie. Ce fut
un temps fort bien employé. C'est tout ce que j'ai oui
de mieux pour l'extreme netteté des sons, dont on ne
perd le plus petit, et pour la parfaite justesse. Son jeu
est dans le genre de celui de Le Clerc, et n'a que peu de
brillant; la justesse du toucher est son fort. A tous
autres égards, l'Anna-Maria des Hospidalettes de Venise
l'emporte sur lui. . .

Page 81/82

Vivaldi s'est fait de mes amis intimes, pour me vendre
des concertos bien cher. Il y a en partie réussi; et moi,
à ce que je désirais, qui était de l'entendre et d'avoir
souvent de bonnes récréations musicales: c'est un
vecchio, qui a une furie de composition prodigieuse.

Mittwoch, 6. Martii 1715

nach dem essen kahm der Vivaldi der berühmte compo-
nist und violinspiehler zu mir, weil es offtmahls in seinem hauß sagen laßen, da ich denn wegen einigen concerti grossi, so ich gern von ihm gehabt hätte, redete
und selbige bey ihm bestellte, Ihm auch weil er unter
die cantores gehört etliche bouteillen wein langen ließ,
dabey er dann seine sehr schwehre und inimitablen
phantasien auf der violin hören ließ, da ich denn in der
näh seine geschicklichkeit noch mehr bewundern
mußte und ganz deutlich sah, daß er zwar extra schwehre und bunte sachen spiehlte aber keine annehmliche
und cantable manir dabey hatte.

Page 85

A quest'ora, di già si dice che la Coluzzi vorrebbe ballare in Venezia quest'autunno, cosa da me non trattabile, perché per la composizione de' balli ci vogliono almeno 16 o 18 giorni, né questa composizione si può fare in Venezia perché ho tutti li ballerini sparsi quà e la, e perché ho fermato per fare questi balli, il Catanella, bravo inventore che molte compose con Madame St. George. Ballando la Coluzzi qui in autunno dovrebbero farsi li balli in cinque o sei giorni, e questo è impossibile.

Page 85/86

Mit der steigenden Erregung des Schaffenden werden die temperamentvollen Schriftzüge von Seite zu Seite flüchtiger. Die eilende Feder hat offenbar den vorausstürmenden Gedanken des an Einfällen unerschöpflichen Geistes kaum nachzukommen vermocht. Immer größere Dimensionen nehmen die Vorzeichen zu Beginn der Zeile an, immer mächtiger ladet der barocke Schwung der Akkoladen und der bis in das nächstuntere System hinabreichenden Endschleifen der Violinschlüssel aus. Viele in der Eile übersehene Versetzungszeichen sind erst bei nochmaliger Durchsicht nachgeholt und aus Mangel an Raum zwischen den Noten über sie gesetzt worden. Und wo es nur irgend angeht, bedient sich Vivaldi einer abkürzenden Schreibweise.

Page 89

Ma i miei musicisti "del cuore" — diciamo così — sono Gesualdo da Venosa e Domenico Scarlatti; poi anche Vivaldi, ma per una decina di concerti soltanto . . .

Page 90

Iseppo, non so il cognome, fratello del Prete rosso famoso che sona il violin.

Page 97

. . . der entrepreneur davon war der auch die oper componirt hatte . . .

Page 107

Il teatro alla moda del Signor Bene satira gentilissima . . .

Page 123

Forte dei Marmi, 8 settembre 1944

Dopo cena ascoltato alla radio l Juditha Triumphans del Vivaldi. che odo musica di questo maestr di un genio sommo, di un'opera Grandissimo godimento.

Sono un profano in materia: non capolavori. Questo, secondo me, è u

Se io fossi musicista vorrei scrivere così come vorrei, artista di altra dipingere come i greci, o, tra i mode Masaccio, Raffaello.

Page 127

Mit dieser Komposition Vivaldis trit Parallelerscheinung zu Bachs Vertra strumentalen Arbeiten auf dem Geb — ein unleugbarer Beweis seiner Ei le Opus des italienischen Meisters al nis des Florentiner Fundes entgegen

Page 129

Un très beau concert d'Instrumen deux heures, dont la Musique, ain Deum, était du fameux Vivaldi.

Antonio Vandini (corretto in Vivaldi) Sacerdote di cui tengono ottime e sinciere relationi. Si manda parte che resti permesso alli suddetti nostri Governatori di valersi dell'impiego del detto Reverendo Vandini in questo nostro Choro per qualche tempo. Sarà riputato proprio con quella mercede, che della loro attentione sarà stabilità, che non ecedi li ducati 40 al mese. Dovendo poi esser reguagliata questa Pia Congregatione della buona rimessa per le figlie in detto così necessitoso esercitio.

non sincere	n.−	
de no	n.1	presa
de si	n.12	

Page 138

Supplico V.E. aver al bontà di farmi avvisato se più si diletta di Mandolino.

Page 139

Si puo anco farlo con tutti gl'Instrumenti pizzicati.

Page 140

Il sign. Vivaldi veneziano ha scritto l'arie per le parole di S.E. Mons. Barbieri che gli ha dati 100 scudi e se li cantano in casa del principe Colonna dove è andato anche l'ambasciatore cesareo . . .

Page 142

In Mantova sono stato tre anni al servigio del piissimo principe Darmstadt . . .

Page 144

Sono stato tre carnevali a fare Opera in Roma . . . ho suonato in teatro, e si sa che sino Sua Santità ha voluto sentirmi suonare e quante grazie ho ricevuto.

Page 145

Il Prete rosso compositore di musica che fece l'opera a Capranica del 1723.

Addi 30 Settembre 1729

Supplicano Gio.Batta Vivaldi sonator di violino gratiosa permissione di star lontano anno uno dal servitio della Ducal Cappella, passando in Germania ad accompagnare un suo figlio, et sostituendo in suo loco per detto tempo la persona di Francesco Negri; hanno sue signorie terminato che sia concessa al medesimo la implorata permissione per anno uno, spirato il quale non restituendosi sarà depennato dal Libro delle Paghe, dovendo però per detto tempo far supplire della persona del predetto Negri, conosciuto che sia capace dal maestro di Cappella.

Page 148

L'Empereur n'a pas été trop content de son Trieste. . .

L'Empereur a entretenu longtemps Vivaldi sur la musique, on dit qu'il lui a plus parlé à lui seul en quinze jours qu'il ne parle à ses ministres en deux ans . . . Son gout pour la musique est très vif . . .

L'empereur a donné beaucoup d'argent à Vivaldi avec une chaîne et une médaille d'or . . .

Page 150/151

La musica: É del Sig. Don Antonio Vivaldi Maestro di Cappella di S.A.S. il Duca di Lorena, e di S.A.S. il Principe Filippo Langravio d'Assia Darmstat.

Illustrissimo Signore,

Pensando frà me stesso al lungo corso dè gl'anni, nè quali godo il segnalatissimo onore di servire à V.S. Illma in qualità di Maestro di Musica in Italia, hò arossito nel considerare che non per anco ie hò datto un saggio della profonda veneratione che le professo; Ond'è che hò risolto di stampare il presente volume per umiliarlo à piedi di V.S.Illma: Suplico non meravigliarsi se trà questi pochi, e deboli Concerti V.S.Illma troverà le quattro Stagioni sino dà tanto tempo compatite dalla Generosa Bontà di V.S.Illma, mà creda, che ho stimato bene stamparla perche ad ogni modo che siano le stesse pure essendo queste accresciute, oltre li Sonetti con una

212

distintissima dichiaratione di tutte l'e cose, che in esse si
spiegano, sono certo, che le giungeranno, come nuove.
Quivi non mi estendo à suplicare V.S.Illma, acciò si
compiaccia guardare con occhio di bontà le mie de-
boleze perche crederei di offendere l'innata Gentilezza
con la qu#le V.S.Illma sino da tanto tempo le' sà com-
patire. La somma Intelligenza, che V.S.Illma possiede
nella Musica et il Valore della di lei Virtuosissima Orchestra mi faranno sempre vive sicuro, che le mie povere
fatiche giunte che siano nelle di lei stimatissime mani
goderano quel risalto, che non meritano. Onde altro non
mi resta che suplicare V.S.Illma per la continuatione del
di lei Generossissimo patrocinio e perche giammai mi
tolga l'onore di sempre più rassegnarmi

Di V.S.Illma
Humilissimo Devotissimo
Obligatissimo Servitore
Antonio Vivaldi

Page 155
Adì deto
Conoscendosi necessario di far che siano sempre meglio
instruitte le Figliole di Choro nelli suoni per accresser il
decoro di questo Pio Luoco; Et essendo vacante la
Caricha di Maestro di Violino
Si manda parte che resti accetato per Maestro di Violino
Don Antonio Vivaldi con l'honorario de ducatti sessanta
all'anno; Sicura questa Pia Congregatione che dalla sua
habbilità sarà praticato tutto il posibile per il buon ser-
vitio di questo Pio Luoco, e per il frutto maggior di esse
Figliole

non sincere   n.–
de no   n.– } presa
de si   n.11

Page 156
. . . Dalla loro esatta scrittura, hora letta s'intende, che
per conservar il detto Choro nel credito sin'hora ripor-

tato si rende bisognoso il provedimento de Concerti da Suono, et espongono l'incontro tengono doppo le molte diligenze usate di haverne due al mese dalla ben nota attività del Reverendissimo Don Antonio Vivaldi come n'hanno sortito due per la corrente festività di questa nostra Chiesa, e però. Si manda parte che resti impartita facoltà alli Sudetti Signori Governatori nostri di poter accordar con il sudetto Vivaldi per il tempo che si tratenirà in questa Dominante, et anco se le sortisse nel tempo di sua absenza, col mezzo delle missioni, quando riusisse di conseguirli senza l'aggravio del posto, perché d'esso siano contribuiti li due concerti al mese che s'essibisce di dare . . . con l'obligo però al detto Vivaldi di portarsi personalmente almeno tre, o quatro volte per concerto ad'instruire le Figlie della maniera di ben condurli, quando si troverà in Venetia . . .

Con li due terzi
   non sincere   n.1 ⎫
   de no   n.– ⎬ presa
   de si   n.9 ⎭

Page 158

Reverendo D. Antonio Vivaldi M^O de Concerti

                De si   n.7   De no   n.4

So torna a ballottar per pendenze

                De si   n.7   De no   n.4

Il loro stile violinistico è insomma assai avanzato, come dimostra la musica del violinista Vivaldi.

Es muß in dessen schon früh in seiner Jugend geschehen seyn, weil er sich so viel erinnert, daß er in den Concerten, die die Singeknaben in Dresden unter sich hielten, die Bratsche spielte, und sichs bey Vivaldi's Concerten sehr sauer werden ließ.

Zugleich übte ich mich auf der Violine und spielte die damahligen Vivaldischen Concerte Auswendig.

Page 159

Denzio berichtete, er habe an Stelle der Giusti durch Antonio Vivaldi in Venedig die Sopranistin Chiara Orlandi und an Stelle Vidas den Tenor Novello engagiert. Mit der Konteraltistin Peruzzi aus Venedig steht er noch durch Vivaldi in Verhandlung . . . Das neueste, was mir zu Ohren kam, war, der mir noch ganz unbekannte sogenannte Lombardische Geschmack, welchen kurz vorher Vivaldi durch eine seiner Opern in Rom eingeführet, und die Einwohner dergestalt dadurch eingenommen hatte, daß sie fast nichts hören mochten, was diesem Geschmacke nicht ähnlich war. Indessen kostete es mir doch Anfangs Mühe, daran Gefallen zu finden, und mich daran zu gewöhnen; bis ich endlich auch für rathsam hielt, die Mode mitzumachen.

Page 159

Vivaldi a fait trois opéras en moins de trois mois, deux pour Venise et le troisième pour Florence; le dernier a . rétabli le théatre de cette ville et lui a fait gagner beaucoup d'argent.

Page 160/161/162/163/164

Le noble *Grimani,* propriétaire du Théâtre de Saint-Samuel, faisoit représenter dans cette saison un Opéra pour son compte; et comme il m'avoit promis de m' attacher à ce Spectacle, il me tint parole.

Ce n'étoit pas un nouveau Drame qu'on devoit donner cette année-là; mais on avoit choisi *la Griselda,* Opéra d'*Apostolo Zeno* et de *Pariati,* qui travailloient ensemble avant que Zeno partît pour Vienne au service de l' Empereur, et le Compositeur qui devoit le mettre en musique étoit l'Abbé *Vivaldi* qu'on appelloit à cause de sa chevelure, il *Prete rosso* (le Prête roux). Il étoit plus connu par ce sobriquet, que par son nom de famille.

Cet Ecclésiastique, excellent Joueur de violon et Compositeur médiocre, avoit élevé et formé pour le chant Mademoiselle *Giraud*, jeune Chanteuse, née à Venise, mais fille d'un Perruquier François. Elle n'étoit pas jolie, mais elle avoit des graces, une taille mignonne, de beaux yeux, de beaux cheveux, une bouche charmante, peu de voix, mais beaucoup de jeu. C'étoit elle qui devoit représenter le rôle de Griselda.

M. Grimani m'envoya chez le Musicien pour faire dans cet Opéra les changemens nécessaires, soit pour raccourcir le Drame, soit pour changer la position et le caractere des airs qu gré des Acteurs et du Compositeur. J'allai donc chez l'Abbé Vivaldi, je me fis annoncer de la part de son Excellence Grimani; je le trouvai entouré de musique, et le bréviaire à la main. Il se leve, il fait le signe de la croix en long et en large, met son bréviaire de côté, et me fait le compliment ordinaire: — Quel est le motif qui me procure le plaisir de vous voir, Monsieur? — Son Excellence Grimani m'a chargé des changemens que vous croyez nécessaires dans l'Opéras de la prochaine foire. Je viens voir, Monsieur, quelles sont vos intentions. — Ah, ah, vous êtes chargé, Monsieur, des changemens dans l'Opéra de *Griselda?* M. *Lalli* n'est donc plus attaché aux Spectacles de M. Grimani? — M. Lalli, qui est fort âgé, jouira toujours des profits des Epîtres Dédicatoires et de la vente des livres, dont je ne me soucie pas. J'aurai le plaisir de m'occuper dans un exercice qui doit m'amuser, et j'aurai l'honneur de commencer sous les ordres de M. Vivaldi. — (L'Abbé reprend son bréviaire, fait encore un signe de croix, et ne répond pas). — Monsieur, lui dis-je, je ne voudrois pas vous distraire de votre occupation religieuse; je reviendrai dans un autre moment. — Je sais bien, mon cher Monsieur, que vous avez du talent pour la Poésie; j'ai vu votre *Bélisaire*, qui m'a fait beaucoup de plaisir, mais c'est bien différent: on peut faire une Tragédie, un Poème Epique, si vous voulez, et ne pas savoir faire un Quatrain musical. — Faites-moi le plaisir de me faire voir votre Drame. — Oui, oui, je le veux bien; où est donc fourrée *Griselda?* Elle étoit ici . . . *Deus in adjutorium meum intende. Domine . . . Domine . . . Domine . . .* elle étoit ici tout à l'heure. *Domine ad adjuvandum . . .* Ah! la voici. Voyez, Monsieur, cette scene entre *Gualtiere* et *Griselda* c'est une scene intéressante, touchante. L'Auteur y a placé à la fin un air pathétique, mais Mademoiselle Giraud n'aime pas le chant langoureux, elle voudroit un morceau d'expression, d'agitation, un air qui exprime la passion par des moyens différents, par des mots, par exemple, entrecoupés, par des soupirs élancés, avec de l'action, du mouvement; je ne sais pas si vous me comprenez. — Oui, Monsieur, je comprends très-bien; d'ailleurs j'ai eu l'honneur d'entendre Mademoiselle Giraud, je sais que sa voix n'est pas assez forte . . . — Comment, Monsieur, vous insultez mon écoliere? Elle est bonne à tout, elle chante tout. — Oui, Monsieur, vous avez raison, donnez-moi le livre, laissez-moi faire. — Non, Monsieur, je ne puis pas m'en défaire, j'en ai besoin, et je suis pressé. — Eh bien, Monsieur, si vous étes pressé, prêtez-le-moi un instant, et sur-le-champ je vais vous satisfaire. — Sur-le-champ? — Oui, Monsieur, sur-le-champ.

L'Abbé en se moquant de moi me présente le Drame, me donne du papier et une écritoire, reprend son bréviaire, et récite ses Psaumes et ses Hymnes en se promenant. Je relis la scene que je connoissois déjà; je fais la récapitulation de ce que le Musicien desiroit, et en moins d'un quart-d'heure, je couche sur le papier un air de huit vers partagé en deux parties; j'appelle mon Ecclésiastique, et je lui fais voir mon ouvrage. Vivaldi lit, il déride son front, il relit, il fait de cris de joie, il jette son office par terre, il appelle Mademoiselle Giraud. Elle vient; ah! lui dit-il, voilà un homme rare, voilà un Poëte excellent: lisez cet air; c'est Monsieur qui l'a fait ici, sans bouger, en moins d'un quart-d'heure; et en revenant à moi: ah! Monsieur, je vous demande pardon; et il m'embrasse, et il proteste qu'il n'aura jamais d'autre Poëte que moi.

Il me confia le Drame, il m'ordonna d'autres changemens toujours content de moi, et l'Opéra réussit à merveille.

Me voilà donc initié dans l'Opéra, dans la Comédie et dans les Intermedes, qui furent les avant-coureurs des Opéras Comiques Italiens.

Page 166

. . . non sarebbe bastante la mia povera penna a fare i dovuti ringraziamenti.

. . . . non ho avuto altro fine in questo maneggio che dimostrarle l'umilissima mia osservanza, e di formare un Teatro compito. Pertanto protesto a V.E. che ci è riuscito d'unire compagnia tale che, spero, da moltissimi anni non sarà comparsa la migliore in tempo di carnevale sopra le scene di Ferrara.

Dopo che per 90 zecchini ho rifiutato di fare la terza opera di S. Cassiano, per avermi, hanno hovuto accordare la mia solita page di zecchini 100; pure Ferrara avrà due opere che figureranno come fatte appositamente, perché tutte adattate e compite della mia penna a soli sei zecchini l'opera ch'è la pagna d'un copista.

Ad ogni modo, se mi sarà possibile, nel fine di carnevale sarò a piedi di V.E.

La Signora Anna Girò rassegna a V.E. gli umilissimi suoi rispetti, e giacché si compiace offerire le sue imperfezioni in Ferrara, la supplica ancora acciò si degni accordarle la di lei validissima protezione.

Page 168

. . . io ho risolto fare nuovi tutti li recitativi, e dare moltissime arie mie a Virtuosi, e già il primo atto è fuori e tutti li Musici prima di partire da Venezia, sapranno la loro parte.

. . . che il Signor impresario sia in punto di mancare alla scrittura della Mancini . . .

Pare che questo sia l'anno degli impresarii di poca prattica. Così sono tutti di S.Casciano, così quelli di Brescia, così questi di S.Angelo, così quelli di Brescia, di quel di Ferrara non parlo.

Questo Signore non sa far l'Impresario e non sa dove si spende e dove si risparmi.

Crederò anch'io che questo sia l'anno degli impresari inesperti.

Page 167

Eccelanza

In esecuzione al mio dovere, spedisco al Signor Bertelli, per consegnare in mano di V.E. il 3° atto immaginandomi che avrà già ricevuto il 2do spedito sabato passato. Supplico la benignità di V.E. di fare con la sua autorità che il Signor Impresario conti subito in mano della Signora Girò tanti li 6 zecchini, che le 20 lire de'copisti che devo avere von tutta giustizia. Sento che l'opera è lunga, ed era certo che un'opera di quattro ore non era adattata a Ferrara. Componendo li recitativi, ho fatto violenza di abbreviarli, ma questo Lanzetti con un ordine dell'impresario me l'ha impedito.

Page 169

Abbiamo fatto sei sole recite, eppure, da conti fatti, conosco sicuramente non perdere, anzi, quando Iddio benedica i tempi sino al fine, sicurissimo il guadagno e forse non poco.

Non è però trattabile di carnevale, mentre i soli balli,

che d'estate posso pretendere a quel prezzo io voglia di carnevale costerebbero a me stesso 700 luigi. Io sono un franco intraprenditore in simili casi, e soddisfo con la mia borsa e non con imprestanze.

Page 170

. . . uomo molto cattivo di sua natura capace d'ogni errore e d'ogni stravaganza.

Eccellenza

Dopo tanti meneggi e tante fatiche, ecco e terra l'opera di Ferrara. Oggi questo Monsignor Nunzio Apostolico mi ha fatto chiamare e ordinato, a nome di Sua Eminenza Ruffo, di non venire a Ferrara a far l'opera, e ciò stante essere io religioso che non dice messa, e perché ho l'amicizia con la Girò cantatrice. A colpo così grande V.E. si può immaginare il mio stato. Ho sulle spalle il peso di sei mila ducati in scritture segnate per questa opera, e a quest'ora ho già sborsato più di cento zecchini. Far l'opera senza la Girò non è possibile, perché non si può ritrovare simile prima donna. Far l'opera senza di me non posso, perché non voglio affidare nell'altrui mani un soldo si grande. D'altra parte, sono tenuto alle scritture, onde ecco un mare di disgrazie. Quello che più mi afflige, gli è che Sua Eminenza Ruffo, dà a queste povere signore una macchia che il mondo non ha loro mai dato.

Sono quattordici anni che siamo andati insieme in moltissime città d'Europa, e pertutto fu ammirata la lora onestà, e può dirlo abbastanza Ferrara. Ogni otto giorni esse fanno le loro divozioni . . .

Insomma tutto nasce per questo mio male, e que signore mi giovano molto perché sono informate di tutti i miei difetti.

Queste sono verità note a quasi tutta l'Europa; dunque ricorro alla benignità di V.E. a ciò si compiaccia d'informare anche Sua Eminenza Ruffo . . .

Ordiniamo, & espressamente comandiamo a tutti, e singoli ecclesiastici di qualsivoglia stato, grado e condizione, tanto secolari, che regolari di questa città e diocesi, & in qualsivoglia modo in essa abitanti, che memori della disposizione de' Sagri Canoni, Concili, & Appostiliche Constituzioni, onninamente s'astenghino dal mascherarsi, dal fermarsi a Saltimbanchi, e Ciarlatani d'ogni sorte, dal trattenersi, e passeggiare indescentelosa dissolutezza in materia simile, specialmente dall'intervento in qualunque modo si sia a Balli, Feste e Festini di qualsivoglia sorte, sotto pena in ognuno de' casi suddetti di scudi cinquanta . . .

Di più mi ha assicurato che starà fermo in tal risoluzione, se gli venisse ordinato dal Papa stesso di cambiarla, e piuttosto perder l'Arcivescovado, che mutare in ciò sentimento, perché crede di dover far così.

Iddio vuole così, né posso altro aggiungere a V.E.

Sua Eminenza Ruffo nulla curando ch'io abbia suonato in Roma, et avanti l'istesso Pontefice in Camera privata due volta, mi fa questo ostacolo, e bisogna ch'io mi aquieti.

Io mai suono in Orchestra, salvo che la prima sera, perché non degno di far il mestiere del suonatore. In casa con le Girò io non stò mai. Le lingue maligne ponno dire quello che vogliono, ma V.E. sà che in Venezia una è la Casa mia, che paga 200 ducati, un'altra molto lontana dalla mia è quella Girò.

È flagellata la mia riputazione in Ferrara a' segno tale, che già negano di fare per 2da Opera il Farnace da me fatto apposta tutto nuovo per quella Compagnia secondo la scrittura col Mauro. Il mio maggior delitto, che dichiarano li miei recitativi scelerati. Con tutto che al mio nome, et alla mia riputazione mi stà avanti tutta un' Europa, ad ogni modo doppo 94 Opere da me composte, non posso soffrire inconveniente simile.

Eccellenza io sono alla disperazione, né posso soffrire che un ignorante simile pianti le sue fortune sopra la distruzione del mio povero nome. La suplico per carità di non abbandonarmi . . .

La somma protettione di V.E. è il mio solo conforto in questo caso e bacciandoli le mani con le lagrime agli occhi mi rassegno.

Page 174

J'ai trouvé, à mon grand étonnement, qu'il n'est pas aussi estimé qu'il le mérite en ce pays-ci, où tout est de mode, où l'on entend ses ouvrages depuis trop longtemps, et où la musique de l'année précédente n'est plus de recette.

Page 176

Zweene berühmte lombardische Violinisten, welche ohngefähr vor etlichen und dreißig Jahren, nicht gar lange nach einander, angefangen haben bekannt zu werden, haben hierzu insonderheit viel beygetragen. Der erste war lebhaft, reich an Erfindung, und erfüllete fast die halbe Welt mit seinen Concerten. Obwohl Torelli, und nach dem Corelli hierinne einen Anfang gemachet hatten: so brachte er sie doch, nebst dem Albinoni, in eine bessere Form, und gab davon gute Muster. Er erlangte auch dadurch, so wie Corelli durch seine zwölf Solo, einen allgemeinen Credit. Zuletzt aber verfiel er, durch allzuvieles und tägliches Componieren, und besonders da er anfieng theatralische Singmusiken zu verfertigen, in eine Leichtsinnigkeit und Frechheit, sowohl im Setzen, als Spielen: weswegen auch seine letzten Concerte nicht mehr so viel Beyfall verdieneten, als die ersten.

Questi generi sono così diversi che, chi è adatto all'uno, non può esserlo all'altro. Bisogna che ciascuno sappia attenersi al suo talento. Io fui sollecitato a lavorare per i teatri di Venezia, ma non volli mai farlo, sapendo bene che una gola non è un manico di violino. Vivaldi, che ha voluto provarsi in entrambi i generi, si è sempre fatto fischiare nell'uno, mentre è riuscito così bene nell'altro.

Page 177

Era parimente convenevole, che ad un Veneto Patricio fosse questo dramma dedicato, impericiocchè non potendo la storia, ond' è ricavata l'azione, che sommamente dispiacere ad un buon italiano, che non sia come tanto sono oggidi, di sua Nazione inimico, facendogli sovvenire, come discacciati gli ultimi Italiani Re, ricadde la misera Italia per non più liberarsene, sotto il giogo straniero, a tale deplorabilissima sciagura solo dà qualche compenso l'inclita Veneta Repubblica, in cui dal suo nascimento fino ai nostri giorni l'Italiana libertà ci conserva, e voglia Iddio sino al finire de' secoli conservarla . . .

Page 179

Rilevandosi la necessità tiene il nostro Choro de concerti si da organo che d'altri instrumenti per poter conservare il detto choro nella stima che si ritrova ed intendendosi pure che il Rev Vivaldi sia per partire da questa Dominante si trova che lo stesso tiene una certa portione de concerti da disponer e sarebe di necesità farne l' acquisto puro.

Si manda parte che resti impartita facoltà alla carica de signori Governatori alla Chiesa e Choro di potter quando do si avocassero di proposito farne l'acquisto con l' esborso in ragione de Cechini uno per uno de questa nostra cassa, e giusto il praticado.

non sincere	n.3	
de no	n.3	perde
de si	n.4	

Page 182
Conduct Vivaldi
den 28.Julij

Der Wohl Ehrwürdige Herr Antonj Vivaldi, Weltl. Priester, ist im Satlerisch Haus beym Karner thor an Innrem
Brand bschaut worden, alt 60 Jahr, im Spitaller gotts-
acker.

Kleingleuth	2.36
Herrn Curaten	3.–
Bahrtuch	2.15
Pfarrbild	–.30
grabstall	2.–
Bahrleicher und Mesner	1.15
Kirchendiener	–.30
6 Trager mit mantl	4.30
6 Windlichter	2.–
6 Kuttenbuben	–.54
Bahr	–.15

Page 183
Lista deren verstorbenen zu Wien
Den 28. Julii
In der Stadt.
Der Wol.-Ehr-würd. Hr. Antonius Vivaldi
welt. Priester im Walleris, H. bey dem
Kärtner-Thor
alt 60.J.

Page 186
Hat keine unserer Konzertdirektionen Lust, die Lebens-
probe auf eins dieser herrlichen Konzerte zu machen?

Page 189/190
La scelta de "L'Olimpiade", fra le numerose opere vival-
diane che si trovano alla Biblioteca Nazionale di Torino,

è stata suggerita anzitutto dalla superiorità del bellissimo libretto di Metastasio (musicato anche da parecchi altri compositori, fra cui Caldara, Jommelli, Perez, ed infine Pergolesi); ma anche dalla singolare bellezza della musica. L'Opera ha tuttavia richiesto un paziente lavoro di adattamento, anzitutto per le necessità di dover ridurre allo stretto necessario i lunghissimi recitativi ai quali certamente il pubblico teatrale dell' epoca non dava nessun ascolto. Mancando poi alcuni pezzi importanti, questi sono stati tolti da un'altra opera vivaldiana: "La Dorilla", la quale fu rappresentata lo stesso anno (1734) sullo stesso teatro di S.Angelo a Venezia. La "Dorilla" è un' opera di cui il manoscritto torinese porta la dicitura: "atti tre, con sinfonia e cori che cantano e ballano", e che è assai più ricca dell'Olimpiade in pezzi di insieme e sopratutto di cori e danze. Donde la decisione di togliere da questa quanto mancava all'Olimpiade, avendo per sè la coscienza di non fare altro che quanto praticavano correntemente i maestri di quell'epoca (nelle mie ricerche alla Nazionale di Torino ho ritrovato una medesima aria in quattro opere diverse di Vivaldi!)

Chi ha avuto l'incarico dell'adattamento e della trascrizione ha voluto fare opera di scrupolosa ed umile fedeltà allo stile originale, senza peraltro pretendere dal pubblico di dover sopportare rigori o convenzioni, oggi indiscutibilmente fastidiosi. Per esempio, il clavicembalo, che accompagna i recitativi, è stato invece soppresso (!) in tutte le arie, il cui tessuto orchestrale integrava da solo l'armonia con buon risultato sonoro. Non tutti i pezzi dell'opera originale erano ugualmente significativi: è stato creduto, quindi, di dover fare tagli, spostamenti e sostituzioni: i lunghissimi recitativi sono stati limitati al minimo possibile, perchè il recitativo oltre una certa misura poteva rappresentare un ostacolo alle esigenze della moderna attenzione . . .

La vita espressiva della musica non ha avuto alcun bisogno d'essere arrichita con timbri diversi da quelli originali. L'ambiente sonoro, quindi, che è parte dello stile, è stato rispettato nelle sue funzioni.

Page 192

Für das vollkommen undramatische "pastorale Drama" das 1732 in Verona uraufgeführt worden war, konnten sich die heutigen Opernliebhaber nicht mehr genügend interessieren, wenn auch die beiden Sängerinnen und die vier Sänger der italienischen Schule alle Ehre machten. Die größten Verehrer von Vivaldi rückten schließlich unruhig auf ihren Sitzen hin und her, weil im Verlauf von drei Stunden sich auf der Szene eigentlich gar nichts ereignete. Auf alle belebenden Zusätze hatte man zur Wahrung der historischen Treue ausdrücklich verzichtet. Nur sehr starke Kürzungen hätten gestattet, sich der musikalischen Qualitäten besser zu erfreuen.

Page 192

Malgré son amour de l'oeuvre, Louis Decreux a dû réduire la partition d'un bon tiers, car à l'époque de Vivaldi le compositeur et son public étaient moins exigeants qu' aujourd'hui. Pourvu que la musique fût de qualité, n' importe quel livret était bon, et celui de Scipione Maffei est à la fois d'une complication extrême et dramatiquement inexistant . . . il y aurait de quoi bâiller d'ennui sans Vivaldi, qui brode sur ces péripéties des airs d'une courbe très pure, quoique d'un lyrisme tempéré, quelques pages d'une noble grandeur qui fait présager celle de Gluck, des ensembles pleins de verve pittoresque, des portraits habilement croqués et parfois ironiques, et des interludes et ritournelles où l'on retrouve son génie instrumental.

Bibliography

Alberti, Luciano: Il teatro vivaldiano e problemi di rappresentazione allora e oggi. In: Convegno Vivaldiano, Venice 1978

Altmann, Wilhelm: Thematischer Katalog der gedruckten Werke Antonio Vivaldis. AfM IV/533

Arnold, Denis: Orphans and Ladies: the Venetian Concervatoires (1680–1790). Proc.of the R.Mus.Ass. Vol. 89, 1962/1963 p. 31–47

Blainville, Charles-Henri: L'esprit de l'art musical, ou Réflexions sur la musique et ses différentes parties. Geneva 1754. German translation in: Hiller, Nachrichten 1767

Bukofzer, Manfred F.: Music in the Baroque Era. New York 1947

Casella, Alfred: Come sono state scelte ed elaborate le musiche della "settimana". (Antonio Vivaldi, note e documenti, Siena 1939/11–14)

—: La settimana Vivaldi a Siena. In: Radiocorriere, August 1939

Cavicchi, Adriano: Inediti nell' epistolario Vivaldi-Bentivoglio. NRMI 1967/45–79

De Brosses, Charles: Lettres familières sur l'Italie (NA Paris 1931)

Degrada, Francesco/Muraro, Maria Teresa: Antonio Vivaldi da Venezia all'Europa, Milan 1978

Dondi, Giuseppe/Balmas, Giorgio: Antonio Vivaldi 1678/1978, Mostra dei manoscritti dei fondi Foà e Giordano. Turin 1978

Dunning, Albert: Some notes on the biography of Carlo Tessarini and his Musical Grammar. In: Schenk-Festschrift, Graz 1962/115–122

Fanna, Antonio: Antonio Vivaldi; catalogo numerico-tematico delle opere strumentali. Milan 1968

—: A proposito del Catalogo delle opere di Vivaldi. NRMI 1969/1246—1248

Farga, Franz: Geigen und Geiger. Zürich ²1940

Federov, Vladimir: Lettres de quelques voyageurs russes du XVIIIe siècle. Festschrift Friedrich Blume, Kassel 1963/112

Fischer, Wilhelm: Instrumentalmusik von 1600—1750. In: Adler, Handbuch der Musikgeschichte. Frankfurt/M 1924/482

Folena, Gianfranco: La Fida Ninfa di Scipione Maffei. Convegno Vivaldiano, Venice 1978

Forkel, Johann Nikolaus: Über Johann Sebastian Bachs Leben, Kunst und Kunstwerke. Leipzig 1802

Gallo, Rodolfo: Antonio Vivaldi, il Prete Rosso, la famiglia — la morte. In: Ateneo Veneto, Venice 1938/165—172

Garbero, Elvira: Drammaturgia Vivaldiana: Regesto e Concordanze dei Libretti. In: Degrade/Muraro, Antonio Vivaldi da Venezia all'Europa. Milan 1978/111—150

Gentili, Alberto: La raccolta di rarità "Mauro Foà" alla Biblioteca Nazionale di Torino. In: Accademie e Biblioteche d'Italia, Rome July/August 1927

—: La raccolta di antiche musiche "Renzo Giordano" alla Biblioteca Nazionale di Torino. In: Accademie e Biblioteche d'Italia, Rome September 1930

Gentili, Gabriella: Le collezioni Foà e Giordano della Biblioteca Nazionale di Torino. In: Vivaldiana I/31—56

Giazotti, Remo: Antonio Vivaldi. Milan 1965

—: Antonio Vivaldi, Catalogo delle opere a cura di Agostino Girard. Discografia a cura di Luigi Bellingardo. Turin 1973

Goldoni, Carlo: Mémoires pour servir à l'histoire de sa vie. 3 Vols. Paris 1787

Goudar, Auge: De Venise – Remarque sur la musique et sur la danse. Venice, 1773

Gradenigo: Commemoriali (MS), Venice, Museo Correr

Hamma, Walter: Meister italienischer Geigenbaukunst. Munich 1964

Hayes, William: Remarks on Mr. Avison's Essay on Musical Expression. London 1753

Hildenfeldt, C.L.: Johann Bach's Leben, Wirken und Werke. Leipzig 1850

Kahl, Willi: Selbstbiographien deutscher Musiker im 18. Jahrhundert, Cologne 1948

Kolneder, Walter: Das Frühschaffen Antonio Vivaldis. Kongreßbericht Utrecht 1952/254–262

—: Aufführungspraxis bei Vivaldi. Winterthur ²1973. English ed., Winterthur 1979

—: Die Solokonzertform bei Vivaldi. Strasbourg/Baden-Baden 1961

—: Antonio Vivaldi 1678–1741, Leben und Werk. Wiesbaden 1965. English ed., London 1970

—: Intorno alla biografia di Antonio Vivaldi. Tavola rotonda sul tema "Il punto su Antonio Vivaldi", Urbino 1978

—: Profilo biografico di Antonio Vivaldi, In: Degrada/Muraro, Antonio Vivaldi da Venezia all'Europa. Milan 1978

Landshoff, Ludwig: Prefaces to the editions of Violin Concerto A maj., PV 228, Ed.Peters 4206, and Two Short Sinfonias by Vivaldi, Ed.Peters 4204. Leipzig 1935

L.P.L. (= Paul Henry Lang), Discussion: Vivaldi, Concertos and Chamber Music. Library of Recorded Masterpieces Vol. 1, No. 1–12. MQ 1961/565–575

Lonchampt, Jacques: L'opéra aujourd'hui. Paris 1970

Malipiero, Gian Francesco: Un frontespizio enigmatico. In: Bolletino biografico-musicale. Milan 1930

Mangini, Niccola: Sui rapporti del Vivaldi col teatro di Sant' Angelo. In: Venezia e il melodramma nel Settecento. Florence 1978

Marcello, Benedetto: Il Teatro alla Moda. Venice 1720

Moretti, Lino: Nuovi documenti per la biografia di Vivaldi. Convegno Vivaldiano, Venice 1978

—: Le inconvenienze teatrali: documenti inediti su Vivaldi Impresario. In: Degrada/Muraro, Antonio Vivaldi da Venezia all'Europa. Milan 1978/26−29

Mortari, Virgilio: "L'Olimpiade" e il teatro musicale di Antonio Vivaldi. In: A.V., Note e documenti, Siena 1939/23−26

Muraro, Maria Teresa: La Fida Ninfa: le scene. Convegno Vivaldiano, Venice 1978

—: Il secolo di Vivaldi e il melodramma: I Teatri, le Scene. In: Degrada/Muraro, Antonio Vivaldi da Venezia all' Europa. Milan 1978/50−65

Nicolodi, Fiamma: Antonio Vivaldi nell'attività di Casella organizzatore e interprete. Convegno Vivaldiano, Venice 1978

Orloff, Conte Grégoire: Essai sur l'histoire de la musique en Italie. 2 Vols. Paris 1822

Pabisch, Hedy: Neue Dokumente zu Vivaldis Sterbetag. ÖMZ 1972/82−83

Paumgartner, Bernhard: Zum "Cruzifixus" der H-Moll-Messe J.S. Bachs. ÖMZ 1966/500−503

Pincherle, Marc: Antonio Vivaldi nella critica dal' 700 a oggi. La Rassegna musicale 1947/302−312

—: Antonio Vivaldi et la musique instrumentale. Paris 1948

Preussner, Eberhard: Die musikalischen Reisen des Herrn von Uffenbach. Kassel 1949

Rinaldi, Mario: Antonio Vivaldi, Milan 1943
—: La riscoperta di Vivaldi nel' 900. Convegno Vivaldiano, Venice 1978
Rüegge, Raimund: Die Kirchenmusik von Antonio Vivaldi. Schweizerische Musikzeitung 1971/135—139
Rühlmann, Julius: Antonio Vivaldi und sein Einfluß auf J.S.Bach. NZfM 1867 Nr. 45—47
Scarpa, Jolando (ed.): Arte e Musica all'Ospedaletto. Venice 1978
Schall, Edgar: Kritik einer Aufführung "La Fida Ninfa". Schweizerische Musikzeitung 1958/353
Schering, Arnold: Geschichte des Instrumentalkonzerts. Leipzig 1905
Spitta, Philipp: J.S.Bach. 2 Vols. Leipzig 1873/1880
Strohm, Reinhard: Italienische Opernarien des frühen Settecento. Cologne 1976
Talbot, Michael: Vivaldi. London 1978
—: Vivaldi und Charles Jennens. Convegno Vivaldiano, Venice 1978
Tiepolo, Maria Francesca (ed.): Mostra documentaria Vivaldi e l'ambiente musicale veneziano. Catalogo. Venice 1978
Travers, Roger-Claude: La redécouverte de Vivaldi par le disque de 1950 à 1978. Convegno Vivaldiano. Venice 1978
Waldersee, Paul Graf von: Antonio Vivaldis Violinconcerte unter besonderer Berücksichtigung der von Johann Sebastian Bach bearbeiteten. VfM I, 1885/356—380
Wellek, Albert: Rangverleihungen unter Musikern nach "Eminenz" und nationalistischen Implikationen. AfM 1966/327—331
Westrup, J.A.: Editorial. Music and Letters 1969/326—331
Zobeley, Fritz: Rudolf Franz Erwein Graf von Schönborn und seine Musikpflege. Würzburg 1949

Picture credits

Virginia Museum of Fine Arts, Richmond, Va.: Ill. 12
Galleria Nazionale, Rome: Ill. 13
Museo Civico, Treviso: Ill. 17
Pinakothek, Munich: Ill. 19
Italian private collection: Ill. 20
Collection Mario and Fisca Crespi, Milan: Ill. 21
Città del Messico, Collection Bruno Pagliai and Merle Oberon De Pagliai: Ill. 23
Pinacoteca Brera, Milan: Ill. 26
Italian private collection: Ill. 31
Accademia Carrara, Raccolta Conte Guglielmo Lochis, Bergamo: Ill. 37
Galleria Nazionale, Rome: Ill. 41
Ex libris Giancarlo Rostirolla, Rome: Ill. 57
The Metropolitan Museum of Art, New York: Ill. 58
Ashmolean Museum, Oxford: Ill. 60
The National Gallery of Scotland, Edinburgh: Ill. 62, 87
Biblioteca Nazionale, Turin: Ill. 65, 66, 67
Museo Correr, Venice: Ill. 71
Museum of Fine Arts, Boston: Ill. 73
National Museum of Wales, Cardiff: Ill. 76
Accademia, Venice: Ill. 88

The following illustrations are taken from the volume
Walter Kolneder: Antonio Vivaldi by kind permission of the publishers Breitkopf & Härtel, Wiesbaden:
Ill. 15, 19, 24, 25, 28, 29, 30, 39, 64, 84, 86.

Index of names

A

Adler (handbook) 186
Adriana dalla Tiorba 121
Alberti, Domenico 184
Albinoni, Tommaso 75, 143, 176
Aldiviva (A. Vivaldi) 99, 107
Altmann, Wilhelm 14, 186
Anna-Maria 43, 67
Aristoteles 108
Arteaga, Esteban 185
August the Strong 63
Avison, Charles 184

B

Bach, Johann Ernst 185
Bach, Johann Sebastian 9, 12, 13, 14, 58, 125, 127, 130, 134, 136, 185, 186, 195
Bach, Wilhelm Friedemann 58, 59, 62
Baduarius, Johannes 34
Baldini, Lucrezia 99
Barbari, Jacopo de 22
Barbieri, Monsignor 140
Beer 84
Beethoven, Ludwig van 62, 195
Bella, Gabriele 161
Benda, Franz 158
Benedict XIII. 140, 145

Benedikt, H. 159
Benincasa 187
Bentivoglio d'Aragona, Guido 12, 46, 138, 142, 144, 165, 172, 173
Bertelli 168
Bertini 185
Bettinelli, Saverio 12, 185
Bibiena, Francesco 109
Blainville, Charles-Henri 184
Blancey, de 40, 81
Bodiani, C. 117
Boivin, Mme. 50
Bollani, Giuseppe Maria 165, 166, 167, 168, 172
Borghi di Belisania 99, 107
Bortoli, Antonio 51, 53, 63
Brahms, Johannes 195
Breitkopf & Härtel 58, 59
Brosses, Charles de 40, 67, 81, 84, 133, 174, 176, 177
Brustolon, Giovanni Battista 45
Bukofzer, Manfred F. 123
Burney, Charles 158

C

Caldara, Antonio 38, 189
Calicchio, Camilla (mother of A. Vivaldi) 20
Calicchio, Camillo (grandfather of A. Vivaldi) 20
Campianu, Eva 194

G

Gallo, Rudolfo 181
Galuppi, Baldassare 38
Gasparini, Francesco 36, 44, 55, 118, 123, 154, 155
Gaviniès, Pierre 185
Geltruda 43
Gentili, Alberto 15, 118, 186, 187, 188
Gerber, Ernst Ludwig 158
Gesualdo da Venosa 89
Ghezzi, Pier Leone 144, 145
Ghignone: see Guignon
Giazotto, Remo 47, 97, 142
Giordano, Filippo 188
Giordano, Renzo 15, 188, 193
Girard 140
Giraud (Girò), Anna 45, 140, 143, 161, 162, 164, 166, 168, 170, 180
Giulia 86
Giusti, G. 159
Giustinian, Giulio 23
Gluck, Christoph Willibald Ritter von 192
Gobetti, Francesco 76, 80
Goethe, Johann Wolfgang von 39
Gofriller, Matteo 75, 76
Goldoni, Carlo 47, 97, 143, 159, 163, 177
Goudar, Auge 185
Gradenigo 12, 181
Graupner, Johann Christoph 124
Grimani 160, 162
Grimani, Antonio 177

Guardi, Francesco 23, 39, 42, 56, 82, 119, 125, 130, 137, 175, 195, 196
Guarnerius, Petrus 76, 78
Guignon (Ghignone), Jean-Pierre 158

H

Handel, George Frideric 195
Hamma, Walter 75, 77, 78, 79, 80
Hasse, Johann Adolph 38, 167
Haydn, Joseph 195
Hayes, William 184
Hilgenfeldt, C.L. 186
Hiller, Johann Adam 64, 184
Hoffmeister & Kühnel 8
Holdsworth 83
Horace 108

I

Innocence XIII. 145

J

Jennes, Charles 83
Jommelli, Niccolò 189
Juvarra, Filippo 147

K

Keiser, Reinhard 129
Kleiner, Samuel 183
Kolneder, Walter 188
Kreisler, Fritz 14, 58, 186

237

W

Wagner, Richard 62, 195
Waldersee, Paul Graf von 186
J. Walsh & J. Hare 47
Wellek, Albert 194
Westrup, Jack Allan 129
Wieniawski, Henri 78
Wright, Edward 91
Württemberg, Duke of 65

Z

Zabaletta 43
Zampini, G. 96, 98
Zeno, Apostolo 107, 129, 161
Zeno, Pier 129
Zobeley, Fritz 10